Cambridge Elements

Elements in Public and Nonprofit Administration

SUSTAINABLE INCLUSION THROUGH PERFORMANCE-DRIVEN PRACTICES

An Evidence-Based, Dynamic Systems Framework

Ruth Sessler Bernstein
Pepperdine University
Paul Salipante
Case Western Reserve University

PMRA
public management research association

CAMBRIDGE
UNIVERSITY PRESS

CAMBRIDGE
UNIVERSITY PRESS

Shaftesbury Road, Cambridge CB2 8EA, United Kingdom

One Liberty Plaza, 20th Floor, New York, NY 10006, USA

477 Williamstown Road, Port Melbourne, VIC 3207, Australia

314–321, 3rd Floor, Plot 3, Splendor Forum, Jasola District Centre, New Delhi – 110025, India

103 Penang Road, #05–06/07, Visioncrest Commercial, Singapore 238467

Cambridge University Press is part of Cambridge University Press & Assessment, a department of the University of Cambridge.

We share the University's mission to contribute to society through the pursuit of education, learning and research at the highest international levels of excellence.

www.cambridge.org
Information on this title: www.cambridge.org/9781009551519

DOI: 10.1017/9781009551540

When citing this work, please include a reference to the DOI 10.1017/9781009551540

First published 2025

A catalogue record for this publication is available from the British Library

ISBN 978-1-009-55151-9 Hardback
ISBN 978-1-009-55156-4 Paperback
ISSN 2515-4303 (online)
ISSN 2515-429X (print)

Sustainable Inclusion through Performance-Driven Practices

An Evidence-Based, Dynamic Systems Framework

Elements in Public and Nonprofit Administration

DOI: 10.1017/9781009551540
First published online: May 2025

Ruth Sessler Bernstein
Pepperdine University

Paul Salipante
Case Western Reserve University

Author for correspondence: Ruth Sessler Bernstein,
Ruth.Bernstein@pepperdine.edu

Abstract: How can organizations better achieve inclusion, equity, and superior performance from diversity? Decades of stalled progress require a wider range of policies. Applying a system thinking approach to a transdisciplinary synthesis of research findings, the authors' comprehensive framework guides inquiry and practice by identifying problematic dynamics. Comparative case studies reveal, in contrast, favorable dynamics of intergroup contact that result from an evolved elaboration of practices for inclusive interactions, socialization, and accountability. Over time, when promoted for mission attainment, applied to all members, and customized to the workgroup, the practices generate inclusion, equity, and superior performance.

Keywords: inclusive interactions, diversity, performance, equity, accountability, anti-inclusive practices, system dynamics thinking

ISBNs: 9781009551519 (HB), 9781009551564 (PB), 9781009551540 (OC)
ISSNs: 2515-4303 (online), 2515-429X (print)

Contents

1 Introduction

Why do group-based economic and social disparities continue to exist in our societies and organizations? After decades of efforts, achieving inclusion and equity with now-typical diversity statements and policies has proven to be what Churchman (1967) would call a *wicked problem*, complex and persistent. This is so for many but, importantly, not for all organizations. Some public and nonprofit organizations have achieved sustained success with diversity. An important goal for research is to identify the problematic phenomena that challenge diversity and how some organizations have overcome those challenges. Evidence strongly suggests that we, as societies, can do better through an informed organizational approach.

1.1 The Opportunity

Repeatedly over time, political and social forces arise that counter efforts to improve social justice. The stark reality in the United States is that economic progress for underrepresented groups has stagnated since the ending decades of the last century. As but one example of findings reviewed next, the Black–White wage gap for both men and women has not decreased but, rather, increased since 1980 (Daly et al., 2017), Taking into account such realities, this monograph presents an evidence-based approach to achieving goals of inclusion, equity, social justice, and organizational performance with diversity. Its analyses identify and deal with continuing social phenomena antithetical to these goals, drawing on systematic reviews of large bodies of empirical research from multiple fields and multiple case studies of public and nonprofit organizations. These bodies of evidence lead to understandings that call for and identify a new path forward in organizations. The understandings are:

1. Contrary to popular opinion, progress on equity and social justice for underrepresented groups in the United States has stagnated for many decades.
2. Long-standing, currently dominant formal policies and practices for increasing representation of underrepresented groups have failed to produce progress on equities at the societal and workplace levels, with many of these practices being counter-effective for those groups.
3. Current political and social realities are but the most recent manifestation of underlying dynamics at societal and organizational levels that continually reproduce social disparities and lost organizational effectiveness.
4. At the workgroup level inclusion of members of underrepresented groups is a key to achieving sustained performance and equity from diversity.

5. Effective antecedents (stimulators) of inclusion are managerial practices typically adopted to increase workgroup and organizational performance. Avoiding the resistance historically engendered by formal diversity management policies, proper performance-oriented practices create task-productive interpersonal interactions among all workgroup members.
6. Differing versions of such workplace practices for inclusion are readily available to fit a particular public or nonprofit sector organization's mission, history, and operational context.
7. "Checking the box" by adopting a diversity management statement and policy is insufficient. Achieving inclusion and equity requires managerial persistence and attention to feedback.

1.2 Research and Practice Issues for Public and Nonprofit Organizations

The findings and conclusions from recent literature reviews and key empirical studies in the fields of public administration and nonprofit governance point to the key diversity issues and challenges facing organizations in those sectors. In the public sector much diversity research has proceeded from a focus on representation, with social justice and effective mission attainment calling for representation in the organization's workforce of populations reflecting the community and client-base being served (Sabharwal et al., 2018). However, such representation, when achieved, has largely been limited to lower occupational positions, with underrepresented groups crowded into lower-level jobs and equitable representation lacking at higher levels in federal, municipal, and nonprofit organizations (Piatak et al., 2022).

Recent empirical studies published in the most prestigious journal for public administration point to the problems associated with this continuing reality and the nature of organizational practices that can overcome the problems. Regarding issues of equity, research on over 240,000 employees in 25 federal agencies finds that "as workforce diversity increases, the perception of organizational justice decreases when the relationship is moderated by an active form of diversity management" (Hoang et al., 2022, p. 537). That is, formal organizational programs to improve workgroup diversity produce unintended effects, leading to lower, rather than improved, perceptions of justice as diversity increases. The authors note that these programs can be seen by organizational members as preferential to underrepresented groups, an issue that is investigated in detail next.

Concerning performance, Sabharwal et al.'s (2018) review of seventy-five years of research in public administration reports "there is very little empirical research that investigates the link between diversity and performance, and that line of work has produced conflicting results at best" (p. 252). They note the "call for more 'practice-oriented' research" and that "existing research has produced little 'usable knowledge'" (p. 253) and report findings that standard diversity management efforts are insufficient to enhance performance, while inclusion in the form of giving employees a voice in decision-making processes does increase performance.

The main theme in the evolving research, then, is that pursuing representation through currently common diversity programs is insufficient to achieve equity and performance. Achieving equity requires that members of all groups receive formal rewards commensurate with their work accomplishments (Mowday, 1991), and this is increasingly seen as dependent on a frequently missing workplace component: inclusion in critical organizational processes (Nishii, 2013) of all organizational members, regardless of gender and race. For underrepresented group members inclusion has been found to depend on personal elements such as the gender and ethnic composition of an individual's social networks within and outside their organization (Jung and Welch, 2022). Our interest here, however, is in practices that organizations and their managers can institute. Hoang et al.'s study of federal employees finds that inclusive leadership practices are associated with higher perceptions of organizational justice, indicating that certain workplace practices can generate inclusion and result in perceived justice. Similarly, contemporary research in local-level public sector organizations identifies several performance-driven workplace practices that are antecedents of inclusion: lived practices for member voice, decentralized decision-making, and teamwork are related to higher departmental-level perceptions of a positive diversity climate (Jiang et al., 2022).

In nonprofit organizations recent research finds that governance decisions play a key role. Public administration literature suggests that, regarding diversity management, the main goal of organizations was to avoid legal sanctions (Sabharwal et al., 2018). Similarly, boards of nonprofit organizations have been criticized for a "check the box" approach, believing that development of a diversity policy was sufficient to deal with diversity issues. By not taking seriously the call to diversify their boards, nonprofits are impeding their board and organizational performance. When nonprofits commit to board diversity with inclusive behaviors and practices, board performance improves (Buse et al., 2016). More recently, Evans et al. (2024) found that visibly diverse boards have more inclusive governance practices, positively impacting organizational performance.

In sum, research in public administration and nonprofit organizations points to the importance of inquiry that addresses core issues and extends the recent promising findings on performance-oriented workplace practices:

- Why have inclusion, equity, social justice, and improved mission attainment remained so elusive, even as many organizations have adopted diversity management policies and pursued representation? What social and organizational phenomena are undermining the currently dominant diversity management programs?
- What board, administrative, and managerial practices in the workplace can counter these phenomena and achieve inclusion, equity, social justice, and increased mission attainment?

Findings and issues parallel to those discussed earlier are also found in research on business organizations (Castilla & Benard, 2010; Dobbin et al., 2015; Kalev et al., 2006; Leslie et al., 2014), indicating that the challenges proceed from social phenomena affecting all types of organizations. Accordingly, insights on the nature of these problematic phenomena can be gained from research published in many academic fields, covering various levels of analysis and types of organizations. The insights can then be adapted to the specific contexts of the public and nonprofit sectors. Here, we draw on our transdisciplinary synthesis of research, reported in greater detail in Bernstein et al. (2022). The synthesis integrates empirical research in the academic disciplines of psychology, social psychology, sociology, and economics and the applied fields of management and organizations, urban studies, and health care, enabling scholars and managers in each discipline and field to leverage the knowledge generated in other fields.

1.3 Motivations for Driving Diversity with Inclusion and Equity

The stakes of succeeding with diversity are high for underrepresented groups, organizations, and society at large. Accordingly, members of nonprofit and public organizations can be motivated by either or all of four arguments, two being fundamental societal arguments for diversity with inclusion and equity and two being organizational arguments for superior mission attainment. The first fundamental argument, the *moral/social justice argument*, recognizes that every individual has value to contribute. From a moral perspective, many nonprofit and public sector organizations are created to improve society and therefore, should be diverse, inclusive, and equitable. The social justice perspective highlights the need to address the barriers and historical factors that have led to unfair conditions for marginalized populations. The moral/social justice argument has become increasingly relevant given the recent political and legal actions taken to inhibit diversity (see Section 10.2). These actions are eroding prior advancements in, and public opinion about, diversity and inclusion.

Second is the *economic argument*, based on the idea that organizations and countries that tap into diverse talent pools are stronger and more economically efficient. With labor economics analyses (Section 3) revealing that progress in reducing race/ethnicity and gender disparities has stalled, the United States is bearing a sizeable loss of economic performance. The estimated annual loss due to deficient use of human capital is on the order of $1 trillion, approximately 15 percent of Gross National Product (Buckman et al., 2021). To remedy this loss, equity and performance can be simultaneously achieved by decision-makers avoiding a *taste for discrimination* (Becker, 1971) and, instead, basing personnel decisions such as hiring and promoting solely on criteria that reflect an individual's actual capabilities for high performance. Adding to these criteria a preference for a particular group dilutes the decision's validity and results in diminished utilization of talent for the organization and society. Workplace discrimination creates further costs for organizations as they expend effort to replace the more than two million American workers who leave their jobs each year due to unfairness and discrimination (Center for American Progress, 2012). Simply, for organizations to be more diverse and inclusive makes economic sense as they leverage the talent pools of different populations.

The third, *client argument* is predicated on the idea that organizations will better achieve their missions if they reflect the diversity of their client base (Ely & Thomas, 2001; Sabharwal et al., 2018). Nonprofit and public sector clients want to see themselves represented in the organizations that serve them, and organizations with representative leadership are more likely to understand and serve their clients' needs well. Finally, the *results argument* is based on the understanding that diverse teams and workgroups have the potential to perform better (Bernstein et al., 2022). Diverse teams can provide multiple perspectives and lived experiences that result in better decision-making and problem solving, finding better solutions to organizational and social problems. However, as we discuss next, research finds that improved performance from diversity is far from automatic, requiring organizations to create particular team conditions to achieve superior results.

Achieving performance and equity from diversity depends not only on the presence of talented, diverse individual work unit members but also on the social practices and organizational values that organizational members follow as they interact with each other to achieve their organization's goals. From our public and nonprofit organizational cases, we identify the value and feasibility of

- pursuing specific practices and values for inclusion and equity of all organizational members, and
- promoting this pursuit as an avenue to superior mission attainment.

Even where "DEI" policies are under political attack, high-achieving nonprofits and governmental organizations can demonstrate to other organizations the performance, social justice, moral, client, and economic reasons for adopting workplace practices for inclusion and equity. However, we caution leaders against promoting these practices to their members as diversity management initiatives. Given the backlash accompanying DEI being politicized (see Section 4) and the reality that teamwork and other performance-driven workplace practices are antecedents of inclusion (Jiang et al., 2022), our case analyses (Sections 7 and 9) find that success with diversity and equity can result from managers and staff promoting inclusive workplace practices for team performance and mission achievement. The mission-oriented logic is a natural fit in the many nonprofit and public sector organizations whose members are committed to attaining an important societal mission. By adopting practices and values for fully including all members in mission pursuit, alert nonprofit and public organizations can both benefit from and demonstrate to other organizations the performance and equity advantages of properly leveraging diversity through inclusion (Bernstein & Salipante, 2024).

1.3.1 An Illustrative Case: Partial Success and Missed Opportunity

Girl Scouts of the USA (GSUSA) illustrates diversity policy logics, opportunities, and shortfalls (Weisinger & Salipante, 2005, 2007). During the 1990s this large nonprofit was among the first in the United States to seriously pursue racial/ethnic diversity, having a goal of membership growth. Among its girl members, although not its troop leaders, it was highly successful in greatly improving the national representation of groups previously scarce in scouting. This approach was similar to compliance approaches centered on improving representation of underrepresented groups, but it largely neglected inclusion. The human tendency to prefer engaging with similar others kept individual troops largely homogeneous, even in racially integrated schools and communities. To overcome this separation, some GSUSA councils created valuable opportunities for differing troops to interact in positive, mission- and values-driven activities at inter-troop sleepovers. However, these opportunities were too scarce and infrequent to achieve any meaningful measure of sustained inclusion. The potential for inclusion and equity from diversity was available to the organization, but a limited policy focus and resistance from some adult members hampered its achievement. This case and others are described and analyzed in Sections 7 and 9.

1.4 Requisite Analyses: The Dynamics of Complex Systems

Across the many academic disciplines that study diversity phenomena, we could find little research that has taken a system perspective on diversity phenomena or investigated dynamics driving the reproduction of diversity problems over time. Given the historical challenges, analyses that examine the dynamics of complex systems (Forrester, 1961, 1990; Mabin & Cavana, 2024; Meadows, 2008; Sterman, 2002) are required to produce relevant knowledge. In contrast, assumptions of short-term causal effects of one or a few actions have proven erroneous over the longer-term. Systems thinking identifies the many factors in play, and dynamic analyses of feedback processes reveal the interplay of the multiple factors over time, pointing to actions that support or undermine the intended effects of policies.

1.5 Evidence-Based Modeling

Applying empirical findings from research studies, we model system processes to identify the *reinforcing* feedback loops that positively or negatively amplify change over time, creating virtuous or vicious cycles. Modeling systems dynamics in this way can guide researchers, policymakers, organizational leaders, and workgroup managers to evidence-based knowledge for effective action. *Systems thinking* is a causality-driven approach to describing interactive relationships among different elements within a system as well as influences from outside the system, allowing for consideration of both internal and external forces. Systems thinking enables one to describe and understand the causality and interrelations between variables using complex models. Within systems thinking we include concepts of *system dynamics* (Meadows, 2008) to emphasize feedback processes among these variables, processes that generate the system's behavior over multiple periods of time. Systems thinking can guide leaders to attend to feedback effects in order to evolve over time a comprehensive set of policies and practices that fit their context.

Our goal is to identify virtuous cycles that accomplish desired goals over time, counteracting the various vicious cycles that have stymied progress. One example is a fundamental virtuous cycle for society driven by organizations' productive utilization of human capital: As organizations succeed in providing more equitable career opportunities and rewards for members of underrepresented groups, those groups have greater incentives to personally pursue and collectively press for improvements in education, training, and other important social contexts, stimulating organizations to make yet more and more equitable utilization of talents from those groups over time.

Systems tools make visible the problematic dynamics that undermine most contemporary diversity efforts and, in contrast, the favorable dynamics that generate sustainable organizational successes in inclusion, equity, and work unit performance over time. Our focus is on the organizational and workgroup levels. Acknowledging problematic factors in the overall society – in educational, community and other social settings – we consider in the following sections well-validated research and illustrative cases that provide insights on how nonprofit and public organizations can productively employ the often underutilized talent available from diverse populations to boost equity and mission attainment, benefiting their organizations, all their members, and those they serve. Recent research on unintended, negative effects of contemporary diversity policies (Section 4) is incorporated in our models.

Using system modeling tools, we specify that the *primary leverage point* for organizations to overcome these effects and succeed with diversity is the intentional structuring of *inclusive interaction practices*, formal and informal workplace practices that lead to inclusive interactions among all members. While our specific diversity focus is on members' gender and race/ethnicity, we feel strongly that many of our analyses are applicable to other forms of diversity.

1.6 A Framework for Inclusive Interactions, Equity, and Performance

We begin with a framework (Figure 1), created and refined by a transdisciplinary synthesis of empirical research, in-depth interviews, and comparative case analyses. In the framework and the breakout models presented in the following sections, all the modeled relationships are based on research literature. Throughout, we have attempted to follow the rule that, if it is not empirically supported, then it is not in our models. However, our purpose here is not to provide all the citations that support the models' relationships. Rather, given those empirically revealed relationships, our purpose is to identify the system dynamics in play and how they shape diversity-relevant outcomes over time. Detailed discussion of the relevant empirical literature, with additional citations, can be found in Bernstein et al. (2022). Here marrying the many findings from that transdisciplinary synthesis with concepts and tools from systems dynamics reveals dynamics that impede or support inclusion, equity, and mission attainment over time.

Figure 1 and those in the following sections use formatting that differentiates groups of individuals and types of constructs, feedback loops, and causal effects. The formatting is defined in Box 1.

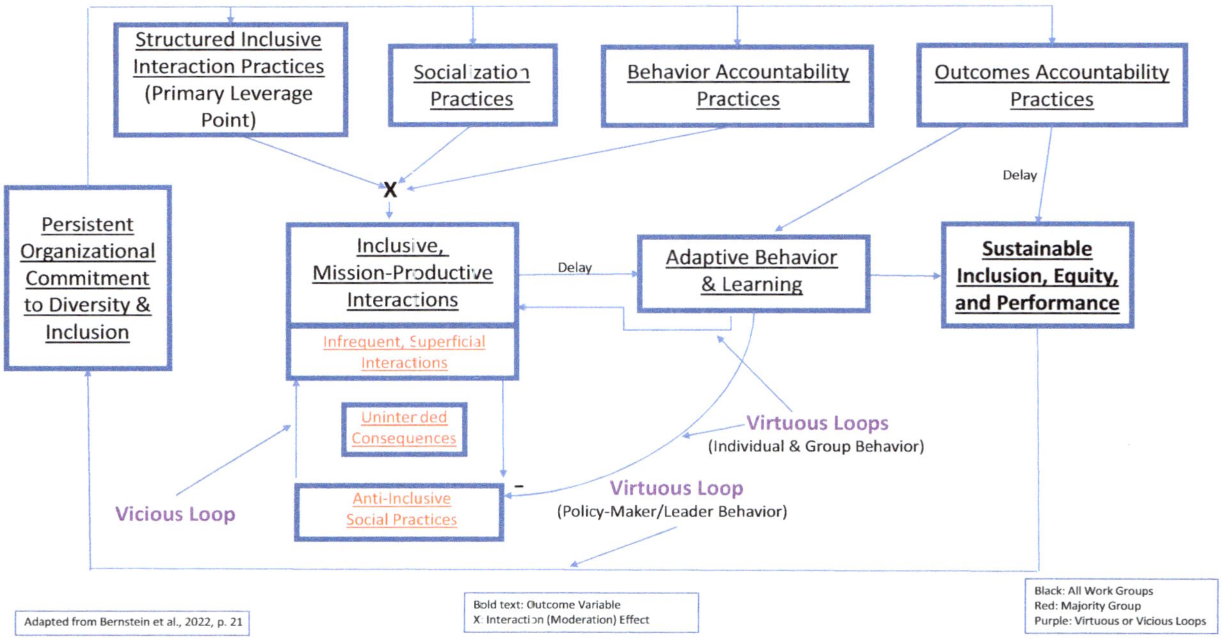

Figure 1 Framework for inclusive interactions, equity, and performance

Box 1 Interpreting the figures

Color coding differentiates three differing constructs:

1. *Black* typeface represents organizational elements (such as the nature of diversity policies and also the workforce in general, both its dominant and underrepresented group members)
2. *Green* represents perceptions and actions of underrepresented group members
3. *Red* represents perceptions and actions of dominant group members

Lines and arrows:

1. In figures with both solid and dashed lines, *solid lines* in the figures represent the findings from the cited research studies and *dashed lines* represent our attempted identification of feedback loops based on other extant research and strongly supported theories analyzed in our prior transdisciplinary synthesis (Bernstein et al., 2022).
2. All lines are positive, unless noted with a negative sign (–).

Other:

Outcome variables are indicated by bold font.
X's indicate interaction or moderation effects
Purple is used to depict the feedback loops that operate over time:

1. *Virtuous*, policy-reinforcing
2. *Vicious,* policy-defeating. The vicious loops indicate the dynamic, self-reinforcing nature of diversity-undermining phenomena

Following the call for a focus on practices, the framework serves as a flow chart. The framework highlights three sets of practices – those for Structured Inclusive Interactions, Socialization, and Behavior Accountability – necessary for enabling meaningful inclusive, mission-productive interactions among all work unit members. A fourth set of practices – Outcomes Accountability – drive Adaptive Behavior and Learning and then Sustainable Inclusion, Equity and Performance. Expanding on *intergroup contact theory* (Allport, 1954; Pettigrew & Tropp, 2006), the Structured Inclusive Interaction Practices are six-fold – pursuing a shared task orientation or mission, mixing members frequently and repeatedly, collaborating with member interdependence, handling conflict constructively, exhibiting interpersonal comfort and self-efficacy, and ensuring equal insider status for all members. These practices facilitate comfortable, inclusive interactions. When combined, these six practices help members overcome three sets of anti-inclusive social practices – self-segregating and interacting with discomfort, stereotyping and stigmatizing, and making decisions based on implicit biases. These exclusionary practices impede interactions and negatively impact performance. Practices for Socialization and Behavior Accountability further foster meaningful inclusive interactions that enable work unit members to challenge their preexisting stereotypes, learn from their interactions, and alter their behavior. Experiencing Adaptive Behavior and Learning leads to Sustainable Inclusion, Equity, and Performance, with Outcomes Accountability Practices further assuring that equity is being achieved. Noted on the framework are dynamics in the form of virtuous and vicious loops indicating where inclusive, productive behaviors are reinforced or inhibited over time.

The framework provides a basis to answer our central question: How can organizations better achieve inclusion, equity, and superior performance from diversity? By applying systems thinking to the various constructs in this framework, we are able to take a deeper dive into each construct to determine where leverage points may exist, where policy resistance may arise, particularly as a result of undesired, unanticipated effects, and how vicious and virtuous loops propagate desired or undesired actions and behaviors. For example, many organizations mistakenly "check the box" on diversity efforts by requiring members to participate in diversity training, training that research finds to be ineffective or counter-effective (Dobbin et al., 2015). It fails to create lived experiences with authentic, inclusive interactions that change attitudes and behaviors. In contrast, the evidence-based framework can guide serious pursuit of inclusive interactions to produce equity and superior mission attainment.

Our modeling, based on extant research, is not a definitive claim of causality but, rather, a call to researchers and organizational leaders to incorporate and evaluate a combination of the promising practices identified in empirical studies and captured by the modeling. Inquiry and policy practice can deploy and benefit from systems thinking, from analyses that recognize present problems and point to alternatives to currently dominant organizational policies. Accordingly, we advise organizational leaders to increase their willingness to pursue, persist, experiment with, refine, and advise and model for other organizations evidence-based policy alternatives that fit current realities and achieve individual, organizational and societal benefits from diverse workforces and populations.

1.7 Reader's Guide

To determine what practices actually achieve inclusion and equity from diversity, along with superior performance, our models follow system dynamics concepts outlined in Section 2. For the subsequent sections, the flow is from the dispiriting findings on processes that inhibit success with diversity to a consideration of more successful processes and organizational cases that illustrate them. The flow of sections is intended to form a logical argument, but we encourage readers to make an initial scanning of sections to identify issues and practices of particular interest.

Section 2: System dynamics ideas on two weaknesses in policymaking and human behavior help to explain the lack of progress in inclusion and equity: (1) not applying systems thinking – the need to acknowledge that multiple cause-effect sequences are interacting in a complex social system, creating a wicked problem; (2) a lack of temporal thinking – the reality that change takes time as a result of delays in responses to policy changes or enactments.

Section 3: Statistics and empirical findings specify the severity and costs of the diversity problem for societies, organizations, and various gender and racial/ethnic groups, contradicting the prevailing social narrative of progress on equity and meritocracy in employment, a narrative found by research to stifle contemporary progress.

Sections 4 and 5: System models based on bodies of well-validated research evidence identify the problematic feedback loops and social processes undermining many current diversity efforts in organizations. Vicious feedback loops operating over time continually *reproduce* failing policy outcomes, disallowing diversity goals to be reached. This *policy resistance* operates primarily through backlash and the perpetuation of societal structures and processes that impede inclusive interactions and equity.

Sections 6–8: The large, well-validated body of research findings on intergroup contact theory point to a more effective way forward through instituting workgroup practices that enhance the productive interactions of all workgroup members, creating virtuous loops fostering over time sustainable inclusion, equity, and superior mission attainment. In Section 7, two cases are presented to illustrate workgroup practices.

Section 9: Comparative analysis of more vs. less successful cases from the nonprofit and public sectors illustrate combinations of effective practices and the feasibility of various types of organizations customizing the practices to their specific contexts.

Section 10: This final section discusses how dynamic system models guide organizational leaders and researchers, emphasizing for the former the role of *policy persistence* over time to diagnose inclusion-related problems and evolve practices that produce a combination of performance and equity, and for the latter the need to incorporate in their analyses the dynamic processes and actionable practices that affect inclusion, equity and performance.

Table 1 Core issues and citations

- What are the realities? Lack of progress – Societal failure to reduce disparities since 1990:
  Daley et al., 2017; Lippens et al., 2023
- Why? Ineffective and counter-effective diversity policies/actions by organizations:
  Dobbin et al., 2015; Hoang et al., 2022; Jiang et al., 2022; Kalev et al., 2006
- System dynamics insights: policy resistance/follow-on effects; leverage points:
  Sterman, 2002; Meadows, 2008
- Continuing reproduction of negative reactions to diversity policies and unfounded beliefs in meritocracy having been achieved:
  Caleo & Heilman, 2019; Dover et al., 2020; Kraus et al., 2022
- What are the underlying social practices? Stereotyping; self-segregating; implicit bias:
  Bertrand & Duflo, 2017; Jones et al., 2016; McPherson et al., 2001
- How counteract? Leverage points residing in conditions for positive, frequent intergroup contact:
  Bowman, 2013; Pettigrew & Tropp, 2006
- How achieve favorable conditions? Cases revealing workplace practices for inclusion and equity:
  Bernstein & Aspin, 2024; Bernstein et al., 2022; Weisinger & Salipante, 2005

Table 1 undergirds the framework presented earlier, summarizing the core issues and selected citations that, when analyzed with system dynamics concepts, provide insights into the lack of progress with current diversity programs and the potential, as demonstrated by successful cases, for achieving sustainable inclusion, equity, and performance through structured workplace practices.

2 System Dynamics Insights for Overcoming Policy Shortfalls

The persistence of the wicked problem of achieving inclusion and equity calls for new thinking if the current disappointing trends are to be reversed. System dynamics offers ways to understand and act on wicked problems that we, as people, typically miss. To explore and communicate these ways, we draw heavily on the work of Donella Meadows (2008) and John Sterman (2002, 2006), work that is rooted in systems concepts developed by Jay Forrester (1961, 1990). We extend their accumulated wisdom on dynamic systems to the challenge of explaining past and current shortfalls in diversity policies. The general thrust of systems dynamics is that intentional policy actions typically lead to a combination of desired and *undesired follow-on effects*. Often, the

Table 2 Section 2 figures

Figure Number	Description
2	Using System Dynamics modeling to persist and achieve policy success through ongoing monitoring and diagnosing of desired and undesired effects.
3	Basics of System Dynamics modeling for achieving policy goals.
4	Competing social practices in the organization support or undermine inclusive interactions, equity, and work unit performance.

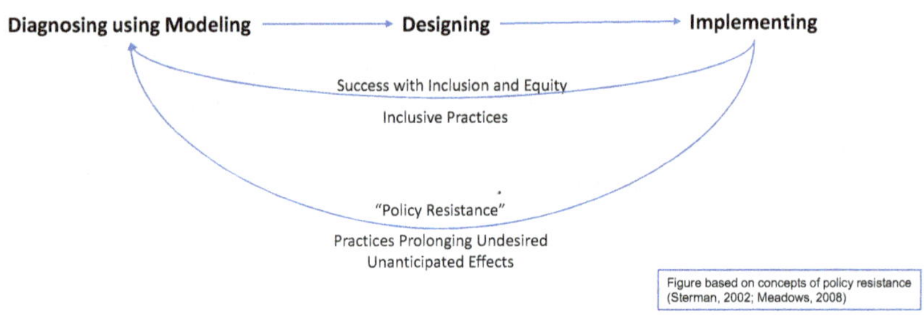

Figure 2 Policy persistence using system dynamics modeling: Continually securing feedback to diagnose, redesign, and implement

undesired effects that follow cannot be readily anticipated. Table 2 provides a list of the figures presented in this section.

A systems-oriented policy that persists over time, as depicted in Figure 2, deals with overcoming the resulting policy resistance. Alert decision-makers repeatedly assess achievement of diversity policy goals, gather feedback to diagnose the problematic practices prevalent in the organization that are impeding better achievement, and (re)design policy elements to strengthen practices for inclusion, equity, and mission attainment.

Based on a career studying global, societal, and community systems, Meadows advises that complex social systems are not controllable but, rather, are inherently unpredictable. They are also susceptible to processes of slow decline in which a system's members become more and more accepting of the problems the system exhibits. Because they face such complexity, unpredictability, and social acceptance of problems, policymakers' short-term and technocratic solutions will fail to achieve desirable levels of performance.

However, on the other side of the coin, social systems are self-organizing. Being unpredictable, they have the ability to create new structures and processes, such as community members coming together to engage in mutual aid in response to a catastrophe. Consequently, systems are capable of producing human benefits that exceed what policymakers are able to anticipate at any one time. While not controllable, systems can be redesigned, re-envisioned, brought into being and evolved over time through human creativity and persistence.

System dynamics enables us to examine the sources of policy resistance, which Sterman describes as how and why "today's problems often arise as unintended consequences of yesterday's solutions" (Sterman, 2002, p. 1). Underlying policy resistance are two broad issues (Repenning & Sterman, 2002; Sterman, 2002). First, complex systems are characterized by feedback loops, the interplay of multiple actors, time delays, and other processes that enable well-intentioned policy efforts to be undermined by the system's responses over time. To aid policymakers, these feedback processes are depicted in *causal loop diagrams*. Second, policy development is flawed by human interpretations and heuristics that are, among other difficulties, simplistic in terms of cause-effect relationships, being subject to multiple challenges. These challenges include: disciplinary, sectoral, and organizational boundaries that narrow our focus; bounded rationality and limited information used for decision-making (Simon, 1996); and a fundamental attribution error (Ross, 1977) of ascribing problems to individuals' dispositions rather than to system structure. For example, ineffective diversity training efforts (Dobbin et al., 2015) persist due to policymakers' simplistic assumptions about the determinants of participants' attitudes and behavior. Another example is that narratives of women's empowerment lead to an interpretation that progress on their inclusion and equality is the responsibility of women changing rather than the need for system structures to be changed (Kim et al., 2018).

The basics of system dynamics modeling are depicted in Figure 3. A model attempts to capture causal effects that operate and shift over time (Meadows, 2008). Inflows of various types – for diversity issues, these are primarily social conditions and associated beliefs, attitudes, and behaviors manifested by individuals – place a system into a particular state. Over time, that state produces characteristic outflows, for example, shortfalls in achieving diversity, equity, and increased performance. Individuals can act on the system based on their perceptions of the system's state, its outflows, and their goals. Discrepancies between outflows, system state, and goals represent feedback that can drive changes in inflows. In a well-functioning system, the feedback leads to adjustments in inflows to produce the desired behavior in a sustained fashion.

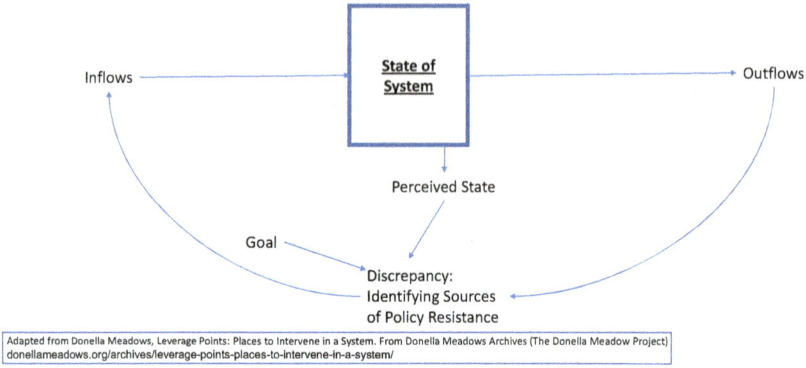

Figure 3 System dynamics modeling

When confronted with a wicked problem, policymakers can use system dynamics models to guide them in identifying system behavior that favors or impedes attaining their policy goals. In Sections 4 through 6 we present such models based on empirical findings from multiple bodies of research. The models focus on habitual practices that members follow and that affect the system's outflows relevant to diversity-related goals. Over time, with persistent commitment, leaders can create new inflows designed to increase the stock of their organizational members' practices (as depicted in the center of Figure 4) that support inclusion and equity and, in turn, work unit performance. To the degree that leaders' inflows succeed, these successes reinforce continued organizational commitment to diversity and inclusion.

However, the new policy inflows form only some of the inflows that the system then experiences, since other inflows are occurring in parallel. As depicted along the bottom of Figure 4, the stock of practices in the system includes ones that resist the intended effects of the diversity policies. These undermining practices are imported into the organization from societal structures and processes that influence how members of the organization think and behave. Following the key understanding from system dynamics outlined earlier, new policy inflows are likely to produce not only the intended results but also unintended effects representing policy resistance.

We can model these intended and unintended dynamics as due to two competing sets of social practices, with each set producing causal loops. One dynamic is driven by workgroup members following particular social practices that reinforce inclusion and equity. The competing dynamic rests on members following other social practices that undermine diversity policy goals by generating effects of exclusion and inequity unintended by the policymakers. Rather than being static, these unfavorable dynamics evolve over time as societal

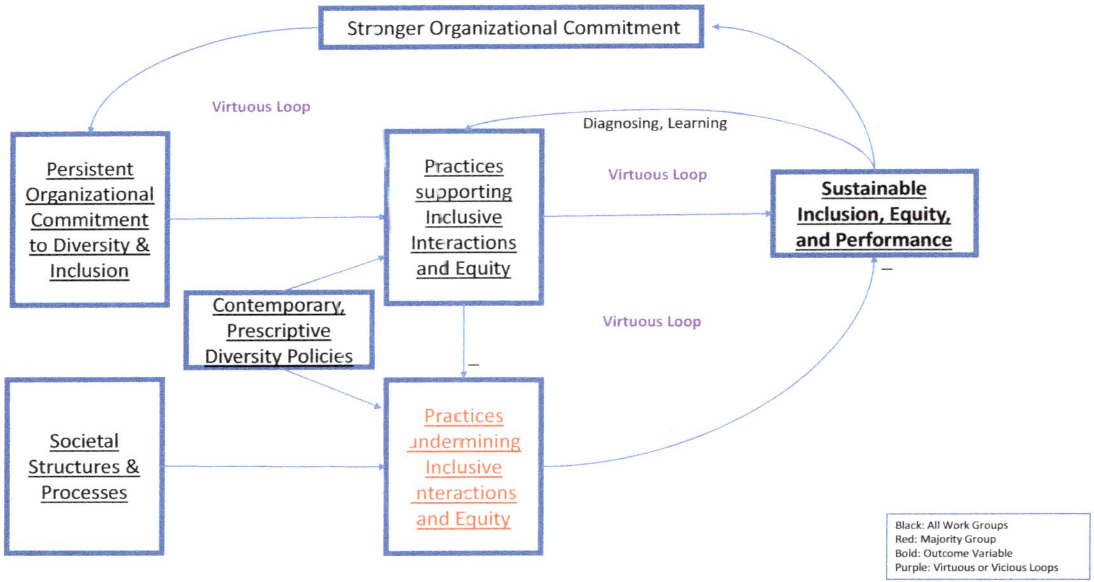

Figure 4 Competing processes for inclusion and equity

events occur, creating an ongoing challenge. Research reviewed in Sections 3 and 4 finds, counter-intuitively, that many contemporary diversity policies contribute to this challenge by driving social beliefs and practices that undermine inclusion, equity, and mission attainment.

With a wicked organizational problem – such as satisfying rapidly changing customer needs or, in the present case, achieving inclusion, equity and performance from diversity – the dynamic evolution of societal issues and associated social practices requires continual policy persistence by organizational and work unit leaders. Alert organizations cannot control this societal evolution but can continue to succeed by adjusting their own policies to achieve sustained inclusion and equity.

To sum up, systems-level analysis enables us to understand diversity policy resistance by modeling and diagnosing a comprehensive set of consequential phenomena that matches a system's problematic complexity. Since the emphasis of systems thinking is on diagnosing the issues as residing in structures and practices, as opposed to blaming actors or events for a current lack of success, leaders can take initiatives to change organizational structures and practices that affect inclusion and equity. As depicted in Figure 2, by persisting with policy evolution based on diagnosing successes and setbacks, leaders can alter the organizational-level dynamics to better achieve inclusion, equity and performance. Diagnosing with systems thinking identifies relevant feedback loops in the form of virtuous cycles that reinforce the intended effects and vicious cycles sustaining unintended effects. Hereafter, these cycles are represented in feedback loops labelled *virtuous loops* and *vicious loops*. In the following sections, we use research findings to identify the elements in these loops. The challenge for leaders and researchers is to identify *leverage points* that drive the feedback loops so we can create and strengthen the virtuous loops and weaken the vicious loops. Systems thinking informs us about the basic nature of less and more useful leverage points, as we consider next.

2.1 Leverage Points

To identify leverage points, Meadows (2008) argues the need to be as awake when engaging with systems as we are when playing a sport or accomplishing a difficult task, "dancing with the system" (p. 170), being willing to let go of our favorite solutions and open to multiple ways of seeing and acting on a system, each incomplete. Modeling a system is valuable in making our assumptions visible and open to critique, but every model is inherently limited. Value lies in bringing together a variety of models from a variety of organizational fields and academic disciplines, as we are attempting in this monograph, and recognizing the variety and varying potency of leverage points available to us.

Meadows (2008) guides decision-makers by listing a dozen possible leverage points, assessing the impact and practicality of each. At the poorer end lies the use of numbers, which she notes can have short-term effects but fails to deal with the system's behavior. A diversity policy example would be a focus on representation with prescriptive targets and quotas for hiring. These have been found to trigger backlash effects, such as beliefs that the hires are tokens and underqualified (Dover et al., 2020). Another relatively poor leverage point is buffers, stabilizing stocks that have the potential to impede unwanted dynamics. Buffers can be highly effective, but the difficulty lies in creating them. Regarding diversity and equity, an example is strong representation of women at higher levels in an organization, a buffer that can mitigate the use of male bias in networking and promotions. The challenge, as we document next, is that attaining a sufficient level of representation at high levels has proven to be unacceptably slow and sporadic across sectors and regions over many decades.

Middle-range leverage points, in terms of a combination of effectiveness and feasibility, including self-reinforcing feedback loops and information flows that drive the system in the direction of desired behavior, "delivering feedback to a place where it wasn't going before" (Meadows, 2008, p. 157). For instance, creating a managerial task force to periodically review organization-wide information and monitor for equitable outcomes, making this information available within the organization, has been found to drive equitable managerial behavior (Castilla, 2015). However, its effects take time to become embedded, due to delays between behavior change and attitude change. Meadows (2008) and Sterman (2002, 2006) note that such delays raise complications for policies, eroding commitment to continue with the policies. Meadows also cautions that some virtuous loops are valuable only infrequently and tend to be dropped due to cost and other considerations, making the system vulnerable to future setbacks.

Among the more effective leverage points is rule-setting. "Power over rules is real power" (Meadows, 2008, p. 158). Those with rule-setting power can create deep system malfunctions or desired system behavior. For example, among our case studies, we found leaders in some high-tech, Silicon Valley firms had values and rules about mission and inclusive behavior printed on employee badges. The badges were then referred to by managers and peers to identify and sanction transgressions. Other rules are central to equity, such as informal, in-practice rules and criteria that managers use for promotions and pay raises (Castilla, 2008, 2015). Differing from formal Fair Employment Practices promoted by human resource staff, these informal rules can produce inequitable personnel decisions.

Shared goals are an important leverage point identified by Meadows. They counteract dynamics that underlie much resistance to diversity policies – namely, groups pursuing their own self-interest at the expense of the collective good, a tragedy of the commons. Shared goals encourage attending to the functioning of an entire system rather than only to the benefit of particular entities. Such goals fit the mission-achievement motivation typical among members of many nonprofit and public sector organizations. For example, we found the value of mission-achievement goals in a research unit in an elite nonprofit health care system (described in more detail in Section 6). Its leader had designed work practices and facilities that would accomplish its compelling, frequently stated goal: contributing to society's physical health by publishing a high volume of rigorous, critically evaluated medical research studies. The goal fit the elite organization's mission and self-concept, motivating all the unit's members to act inclusively with each other and other members of the organization while producing personal satisfaction and career benefits for themselves.

The medical research unit's elite self-concept is an example of another powerful leverage point noted by Meadows – paradigms. Members' social construction of their reality as an elite unit produced sustained commitment to leveraging all members' talents to achieve its highly valued mission. Conversely, in many other situations, a socially constructed paradigm that carries negative group-based stereotypes of inferior talent and competence for underrepresented groups impedes performance and undermines inclusion and equity. Current diversity policies, such as diversity training, are found to have failed in changing these social constructions. We identify leverage points that have proven to shift that paradigm by influencing how members of differing groups interact with each other over time.

3 Policy Shortfalls: Realities vs. Beliefs about Equity and Performance

The previous analyses help us realize that many leverage points are available, some more powerful than others, some more difficult to implement than others. Leaders' motivation to access and experiment with these points should be based on a realistic assessment of their organization's degree of success with gaining performance and equity from diversity. Countering a misplaced belief in progress, knowledge of societal trends gives us pause and spurs that motivation.

3.1 Sustained and Costly Policy Shortfalls That Inhibit Inclusion, Equity, and Performance

That achieving inclusion, equity and performance from a diverse workforce has proven to be a wicked problem, complex and persistent, is made clear by statistical analyses of trends in the United States. The large annual losses to Gross National Product noted earlier have, apparently, not provided sufficient motivation for an effective societal response to the problem's complexity. U.S. national statistics on wage gaps and employment at higher organizational levels show improvements for underrepresented groups in the decades immediately following passage of the Equal Employment Opportunity Act in 1972, but since then there has been little progress and even regression for some groups. For example, reductions in occupational segregation occurred among Blacks, Hispanics, and women from 1966 to 1980, but from then into this century only for women (Tomaskovic-Devey et al., 2006). These trends continue to the present day with stagnation since 1990 in reducing wage disparities (Daly et al., 2017), and an analytic review of studies from 2005 to 2020 showing no evidence of a decline in hiring discrimination (Lippens et al., 2023).

These dual issues of equity and performance confront organizations as workforce diversity and migrations rise, not only in North America but globally. Race/ethnicity and gender differences among an organization's members create the potential for either an increase or decrease in performance. As captured in the Categorization-Elaboration Model (van Knippenberg et al., 2004), decreased performance can result from tensions due to categorizing (negatively stereotyping) differing others, while the potential for higher performance rests on constructive handling of differences in perspectives and the elaboration of information for better decision-making. The competition between these two processes has proven, to the present time, to be "a wash": A systematic review of empirical research shows that diversity has an equal potential to raise or lower team performance (Joshi & Roh, 2009).

Achieving the potential for organizational and economic gain from diversity is, then, problematic, far from automatic. Success requires a shift in focus from mere *representation* of underrepresented groups to their *inclusion* (Nishii, 2013) in productive work relationships, inclusion being a path to more effective human capital utilization. A similar theme emerges from longitudinal research on a large sample of major U.S. corporations, revealing that several well-intended diversity management initiatives designed to improve equity, counter-intuitively do the opposite (Dobbin et al., 2015; Kalev et al., 2006). Practices found to be ineffective, even detrimental to many underrepresented groups, include mandatory diversity awareness training and several fair employment practices such as job tests for promotions. These findings call for improved policymaker knowledge and organizational practices to counter backlash that these practices trigger among coworkers, impeding inclusion (Brannon et al., 2018). Theories of social behavior identify several sources of backlash among members of dominant groups: perceived restriction of autonomy; preference for the current situation and a colorblind perspective; and beliefs that social equalities have been achieved (Brannon et al., 2018). Beliefs that employment equity has been reached through our organizations having meritocratic reward systems are especially problematic (Castilla & Benard, 2010). The belief in meritocracy affects not only workgroup members but also organizational leaders who then feel little need to identify and pursue prejudices and inequities.

3.2 Prevalent Inaccurate Beliefs about Inequalities and Meritocracy

At a societal level, then, two competing explanations reflect differing beliefs, often exacerbated by political debates, concerning the source of inequalities in employment and earnings:

1) Underrepresented groups are receiving the wages and occupational positions that they merit. There is inequality but equity due to meritocracy in the ways that the labor market and organizations allocate rewards.
2) Societal dynamics continue to exist that inhibit equity. Meritocracy has not been achieved.

These differing beliefs center on meritocracy and equity. If the first explanation is correct, differences in preparation (qualifications) for higher-level occupations account fully for inequalities in occupational and income attainment, such as the crowding of some groups into lower-level occupations. The differences can be due to personal choices and/or structural inequities in societal institutions. Logics that favor the personal choice explanation include women's higher involvement in family-raising, causing interruptions in career progress. For example, research has identified gender differences in work preferences at various life stages, with women tending to favor family balance issues more at early life stages and men favoring these issues at later life stages (Mainiero & Gibson, 2018). The explanation of structural inequities is supported by research on the American educational system. Lower graduation rates of women and other underrepresented group members pursuing STEM degrees, particularly in engineering and math, are associated with everyday practices in STEM education, such as grading on a curve to weed out a fixed percentage of students regardless of their relative performance (Museus et al., 2011). Existence of disparities due to such practices and, most importantly, the possibilities for ameliorating them are supported by the dramatically higher graduation rates of STEM-educated Blacks at historically Black colleges and universities (McGee, 2020).

If the second explanation is correct – that contemporary dynamics continue to inhibit equity – we should see differences in employment decisions that reflect bias against underrepresented groups, the "taste for discrimination" that Becker (1971) phrased. Powerful evidence for this explanation comes from audit studies that continue to show bias in hiring. These studies have repeatedly found differential callbacks from job applications sent to employers, applications that are experimentally manipulated to be equivalent in qualifications (Bertrand & Duflo, 2017). Worse, audit studies are likely to underestimate discrimination since callbacks are largely determined by human resource management staff generally attuned to legal issues of discrimination, while biased decisions have been found to reside heavily in the discretion allowed managers on final personnel decisions (Castilla, 2008).

This demonstrated persistence of hiring discrimination belies common beliefs in meritocracy (Amis et al., 2020). As examined next in Section 4, beliefs in meritocracy produce greater discrimination (Castilla & Benard, 2010). Contemporary research, then, reveals widespread public beliefs in a narrative of diversity progress, with this narrative driving a resistance to diversity efforts (Kraus et al., 2022).

A systems thinking perspective encourages us to ask: What effects does continuing discrimination in hiring, pay, and advancement produce over time? As we discuss more fully in the following sections, discrimination feeds a self-fulfilling prophecy of lack of talent, connecting the two competing explanations outlined earlier. One dynamic forming a vicious loop is as follows: The likelihood of discrimination against underrepresented group members decreases their economic incentives to invest in the education and training that leads to higher occupational outcomes; over time, this economically rational behavior of groups experiencing discrimination leads to their possessing inferior qualifications, reinforcing beliefs that their lesser employment outcomes are merited due to a lack of talent, competence, and motivation. Consequently, a failure to make equitable personnel decisions at the organizational level feeds stereotypes at the societal level that see and sustain inequalities as merited. Organizations that succeed with inclusion and equity can help in eroding this self-fulfilling vicious process since inclusive, fair treatment increases the incentives for self-investment.

Next we further address the implications of not addressing workplace inequities.

3.3 Implications for Policies, Leaders, and Researchers

Progress on inclusion, equity, and performance has been disappointing overall. That disparities in employment are due, in part, to disparities in other parts of society, such as education, is not an excuse for overlooking bias and discrimination in our organizations and failing to make mission-attaining use of all organizational members' human capital. As noted earlier, for most underrepresented groups overall progress in employment has ceased since the 1980s and 1990s. Where progress has continued, it has varied across groups, fields and organizations, calling for leaders and researchers to assess the nature of shortfalls to be addressed in their context. For example, women's representation in medical schools and medical practice has improved dramatically over decades. However, in academic medicine, analyses indicate that retention and attaining of leadership positions has lagged and gender disparities in pay have not improved since 1995 (Carr et al., 2015). More broadly, for women in STEMM (Science, Technology, Engineering, Mathematics, and Medicine), a consensus report by the National Academies of Sciences, Engineering, and Medicine included among its conclusions that "Bias, discrimination, and harassment are major drivers of the underrepresentation of women . . .; they are often experienced more overtly and intensely by women of intersecting identities (e.g., women of color, women with disabilities, . . . " (Bear et al., 2020).

The challenge for policymakers, organizational leaders, and researchers is to identify the severity and nature of the diversity problems faced in their setting, seeking practical knowledge on policy-undermining dynamics that apply to their context, as we discuss next in Sections 4 and 5, and on practices that aid rather than detract from achieving inclusion, equity, and performance, as discussed in Sections 6 through 9.

4 Dynamics Undermining Diversity Policy Efforts

Organizational policies must do justice to the scope and complexities of phenomena that, over time, limit and undermine success in achieving inclusion, equity, and organizational performance. Building on research evidence from prior decades, recent literature reviews and studies are identifying a variety of persistent system dynamics that produce unintended, undesired diversity consequences in our organizations. The figures included in this section are listed in Table 3.

Table 3 Section 4 figures

Figure Number	Description
5	The dynamics of intended and unintended effects of reducing barriers to women's entrepreneurship, identifying negative effects on women who do not become entrepreneurs.
6	Common diversity policies trigger unintended interpretations that reinforce anti-inclusive social practices and infrequent, superficial diversity interactions, producing a vicious cycle in workgroups that reduces workgroup performance, inclusion, and equity.
7	Fairness signals of traditional diversity policies generate perceptions of meritocracy that, among underrepresented groups, support several positive outcomes and, among dominant groups, produce several negative outcomes including inattention to discrimination, derogation of claimants, and dominant group members claiming reverse discrimination.
8	Diversity training triggers competing dynamics. Two virtuous loops increase women's advancement to high level positions, while numerous vicious loops undermine their advancement and earnings through interpretations by the dominant group that increase gender stereotyping and biased personnel decisions.

4.1 Modeling Dynamics of Unintended Consequences

As an initial illustration of complexities and unintended consequences, consider findings from a recent empirical study investigating the effects of policies that lower the barriers to entrepreneurship (Castellaneta et al., 2020, p. 1274):

> We propose that institutions that reduce barriers to entrepreneurship lead to intended consequences, increasing entry rates among individuals facing obstacles to entrepreneurship, such as women. But these regulations also have unintended consequences, decreasing the value appropriated by women who stay in paid employment, as these women lose support of their departing peers. . . . These effects are amplified for women in managerial positions who benefit if they leave but lose if they stay.

The dynamics of these intended and unintended effects are modeled in Figure 5. To the aforementioned findings (solid lines) we add a feedback loop (dashed lines) to capture follow-on effects of loss of support and lowered pay causing more women to leave the organization, creating yet less support for women who remain, with this vicious cycle repeating over time.

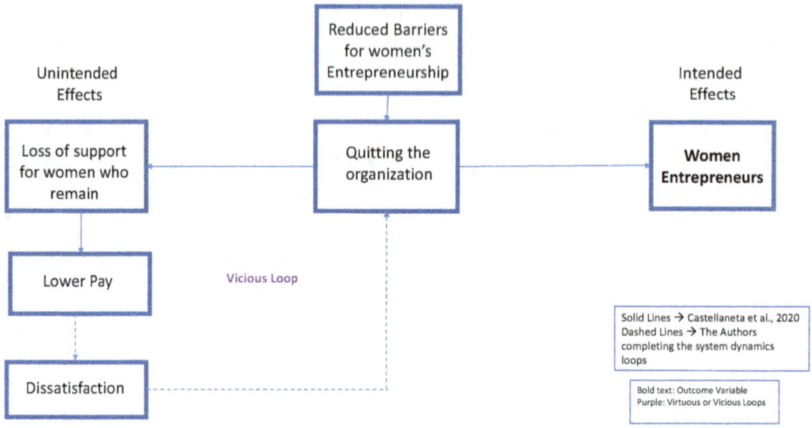

Figure 5 The intended and unintended effects of entrepreneurship policies: Problems for employed women

This phenomenon of a mixture of intended and unintended follow-on effects is but one example of system complexities that confound diversity policies. The complexities produce not only desired but also undesired dynamics that, over time, limit and undermine success in achieving inclusion, equity, and higher mission attainment. Increasingly, research studies are identifying a variety of system dynamics that are producing unintended, policy-undermining consequences in our organizations. Here, we draw on their findings as well as research-based evidence from prior decades that provides insights into the social system complexities that confound contemporary efforts to achieve inclusion, equity, and performance from diversity. By modeling the variety of system dynamics in play, we demonstrate how complex and problematic these dynamics are. However, fortunately, modeling also points to leverage points for effective policies (Meadows, 2008). In later sections we identify and model successful organizational policies that deal with these system complexities to produce inclusion, equity and high performance from diversity.

4.2 Findings on Unintended Effects of Contemporary Diversity Policies

Resistance to diversity policies is driven by interpretations that members draw from their organization's diversity efforts. A meta-analysis of 110 studies (Harrison et al., 2006) found strong Black–White differences in supportive vs. unsupportive attitudes for diversity programs. The more prescriptive the program for achieving equality in personnel outcomes, the greater the differences in attitudes, with the differences in lack of support being four times greater for the most vs. least prescriptive programs.

The findings from this and similar research are modeled in a general fashion in Figure 6, with unintended interpretations triggered by diversity programs leading to interpersonal behavior that, among other negative impacts, reinforces a vicious loop in workgroups. That loop is driven by the *anti-inclusive social practices* (such as stereotyping and stigmatizing) that are imported from the broader society and followed by some or many members of the organization. These practices, and the infrequent, superficial interactions that they produce, reinforce each other, with this vicious loop hampering inclusion, equity, and work unit performance.

The left side of Figure 6 highlights the counterintuitive findings from two highly informative studies that examine a range of unintended effects caused by contemporary diversity policies. First, a literature review of social psychology studies (Dover et al., 2020) identifies the de facto, signals, often unintended, that commonly implemented diversity initiatives send to organizational members. These signals trigger individuals' interpretations of those efforts, some of which initiate and sustain resistance to the organization's diversity policies. Second, Caleo and Heilman (2019) extensively review studies identifying processes that undermine three common diversity efforts – diversity training, emphasizing successes with diversity, and unbiased evaluation procedures – designed to counter gender bias. Contrary to expectations, Caleo and Heilman found that these efforts produced follow-on effects that sustain stereotyping and biased behavior and decisions.

Illustrating the types of dynamic phenomena creating resistance to diversity policies, Figures 7 and 8 are breakout models that detail two examples of the unintended effects found in these recent reviews of empirical studies. First, modeled from Dover et al.'s (2020) literature review, Figure 7 depicts the unintended effects of fairness signals sent by diversity programs or initiatives. When reading these figures, note that solid lines represent the literature review's findings, while the dashed lines represent our' completion of feedback loops, with all lines reflecting research-based evidence.

In Figure 7, an important dynamic is that fairness signals sent as part of an organization's diversity policies for fair employment practices (such as job tests for hiring or promoting) increase perceptions of the organization being meritocratic. These perceptions create positive effects of increased job satisfaction and commitment for underrepresented group members, providing a positive effect on their retention. However, among other organizational members, the signals tend to be interpreted in ways that lead to inattention to discrimination. The interpretations include majority group members being less sensitive to issues of unfairness and to claims of discrimination, and being more sensitive to discrimination against their (majority) group. Follow-on effects then include

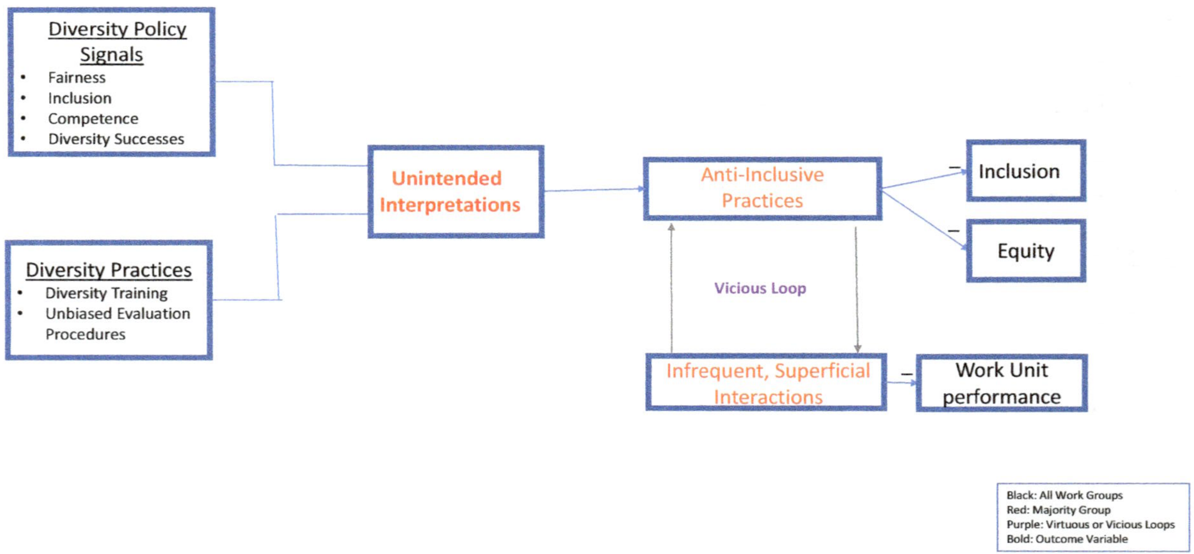

Figure 6 Unintended consequences of common diversity policies and practices

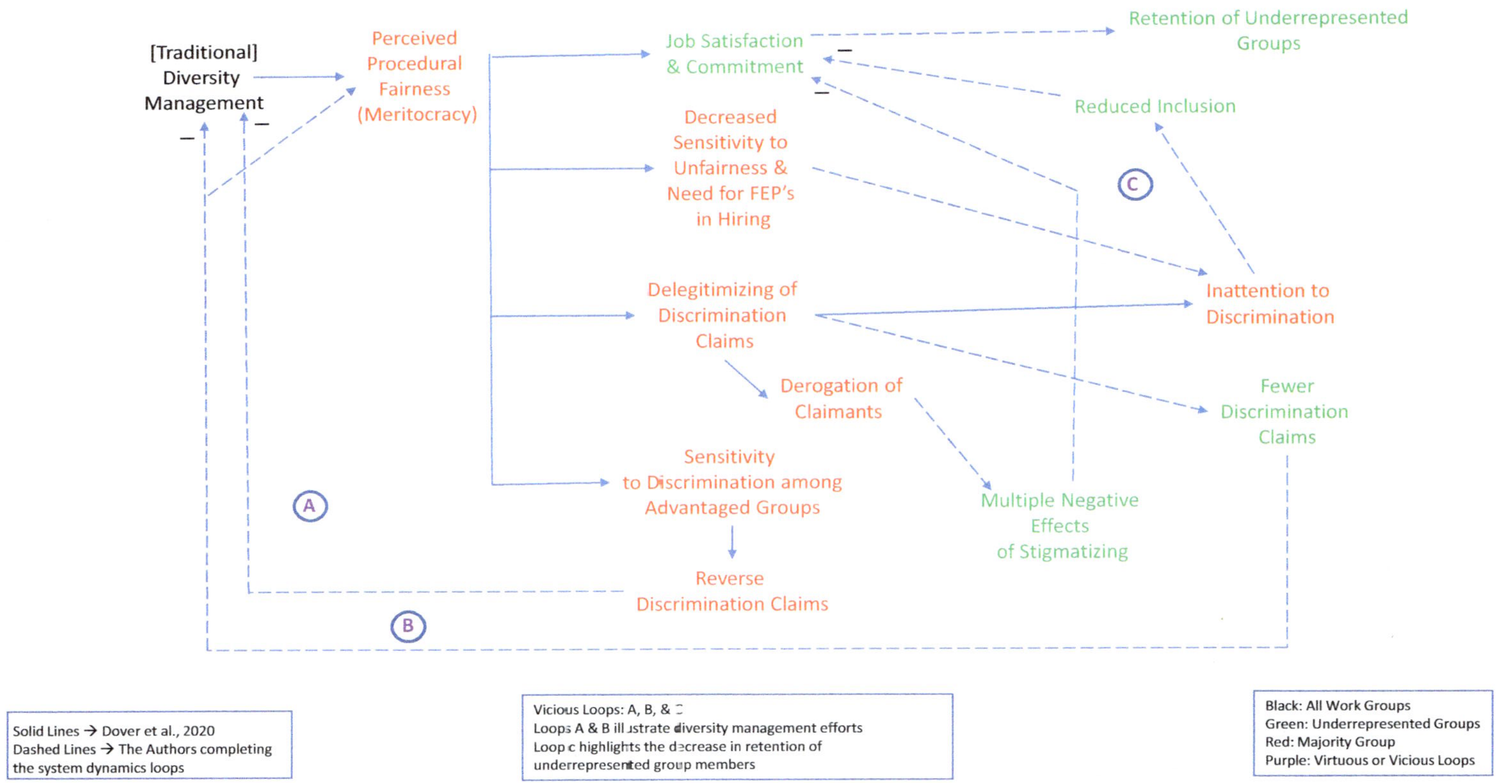

Figure 7 Effects of fairness signals from diversity initiatives

the delegitimizing of discrimination claims by members of underrepresented groups and derogation of those claimants.

Based on other bodies of research, we model in Figure 7 several feedback effects of these member interpretations, depicted as three vicious loops labelled A, B, and C. The effects include a weakening of diversity management efforts and, among underrepresented groups, reduced job satisfaction due to being stigmatized and excluded, and a reduction in discrimination claims. The delegitimizing of discrimination claims and the resulting inattention to discrimination lowers the inclusion and job satisfaction of underrepresented groups, creating a downward effect on their retention. Among dominant groups the reduction in discrimination claims feeds back to sustain perceptions of meritocracy and to support the perceived adequacy of the current diversity efforts. Perceived adequacy hampers the policy-persisting diagnosing and redesigning (Figure 2, Section 2) required to evolve effective policies. Over time, the various feedback effects create a self-reinforcing, policy-defeating cycle.

In sum, the intended equity effects of diversity and equity efforts such as fair employment practices are countered by workgroup members' interpretations that claims of unfairness by underrepresented members are unjustified, leading to behaviors that erode diversity management and the inclusion and retention of underrepresented group members. Dover et al. (2020) further examined the impact of inclusion and competence signals with similar outcomes of good intentions resulting in negative unintended consequences.

Unintended effects of diversity policies are similarly specified in Caleo and Heilman's (2019) wide-ranging review of studies, identifying processes that undermine three common diversity efforts designed to counter gender bias: diversity training; emphasizing successes with diversity; and unbiased performance evaluation procedures. An example of the follow-on effects of these diversity policies is modeled in Figure 8.

In Figure 8 several aspects of diversity training produce a combination of intended and unintended effects through their influence on gender-based stereotyping. Regarding favorable effects, emphasizing the communal aspects of the organization's jobs favors the advancement of more women to high level positions, which reinforces their communal aspects, creating a virtuous loop. Further, an increased number of women in top positions feeds another virtuous loop, with more mentoring reducing anxieties experienced by women at lower levels, reducing their probability of quitting and increasing their likelihood of advancing to high levels, an example of a system buffer (Meadows, 2008). Also, driving the intended result of decreased gender stereotyping is diversity training that emphasizes the value of perspective-taking (lower-left of the figure) – that is, how differing individuals take differing perspectives to interpret a particular

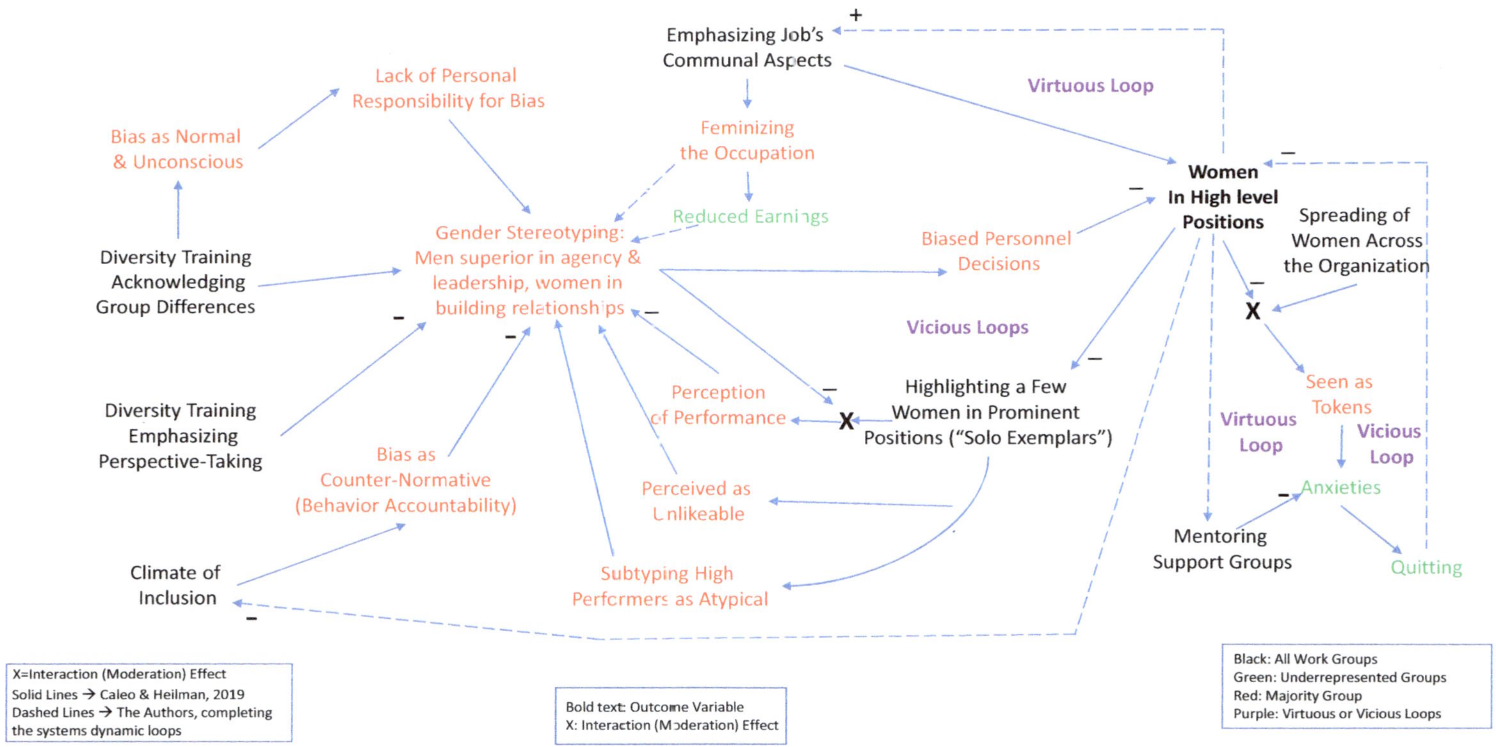

Figure 8 Gender stereotyping: Competing phenomena affect gender stereotyping and advancement to high positions over time

situation, leading to the elaboration of information (van Knippenberg et al., 2004) and fuller knowledge of the situation.

In contrast, training acknowledging group differences (upper-left of figure) reinforces attitudes that bias is normal and unconscious, reducing individuals' felt responsibility for having bias, thereby sustaining gender-based stereotyping. Several vicious loops proceed from the gender stereotyping (right side of figure). One is that biased personnel decisions by managers, sustained by gender stereotyping, constrain the number of women advanced to high level positions, eroding that diversity-favoring buffer. When diversity policy highlights the success of those few women, members tend to interpret those high performers as atypical, sustaining their gender stereotypes of women as inferior to men at leadership. Further (right side of figure), if the organization spreads the few high-level women across the organization, they tend to be seen as tokens, increasing their anxieties and quit rates and decreasing their numbers at top levels. The resulting vicious cycle is then driven by a decreased climate for inclusion (bottom-left of figure) that enables the organization's members to maintain their gender stereotypes. Dover et al. (2020) confirmed these findings by illustrating that the stereotype threat of stigmatizing leads not only to anxieties but also to diminished assessments of one's self-competence, an additional negative impact on underrepresented group members.

In addition, Caleo and Heilman's review examined organizational policy that emphasizes its successes with diversity. These publicized successes help in leaders' persisting with accountability procedures that make managers' personnel decisions more visible. Especially when combined with individuals' desires to present themselves positively and with norms that proscribe uncivil behavior, this visibility tends to reduce members' overt discriminatory behavior. These are the types of effects desired and anticipated by policy leaders. However, less desirable and likely to be anticipated are other effects. The policies may shift discrimination from overt to more subtle, less visible behavior, as also noted in Dover et al.'s (2020) review. The consequences are important: A meta-analysis of empirical studies finds that subtle discrimination produces greater inequities than does overt discrimination (Jones et al., 2016).

An additional finding reported by Caleo and Heilman as increasing the likelihood of discrimination is superiors stating justifications for discriminatory behavior, which tends to legitimize managers' engaging in such behavior even when it is overt, and more likely to be overlooked when it is subtle. Triggered by an emphasis on diversity success are two other factors that shelter discriminating behavior: members believing that the organization is procedurally fair (mirroring other findings on the undermining effects of beliefs in meritocracy) and its members are unbiased. Caleo and Heilman further found that unintended effects can be engendered by individuals tasked with making personnel evaluations. When members of underrepresented groups are the evaluators, others are more likely to see the evaluations as unfair, biased toward those groups. Those others reduce their diversity-valuing behavior, increasing the likelihood of their making biased evaluations. Another unintended effect is triggered by unbiased evaluation procedures, a fair employment practice that requires evaluators to engage in additional, more conscious thinking. These procedures can create cognitive strain that encourages evaluators to short-cut the evaluation process and rely instead on stereotypes, sustaining biased decisions. However, once recognized, these unintended effects can be countered by selecting evaluators with a high need for cognition and by training evaluators on the use of evaluation tools, reducing the strain that they experience.

The confounding overall finding from these two reviews of research is that explicitly labelled diversity policies themselves tend to reinforce various attitudes and behavior, both overt and subtle, that are discriminatory and lead to inequitable outcomes, such as lack of women advancing to executive positions, and to self-fulfilling prophecies of low competence that erode individual and group performance over time. These dynamics fit Meadows' (2008) analysis of systems that experience and then accept slow declines in policy effectiveness and performance. Even in the breakout models earlier, the causal relationships are complex and not obvious, contrasting with the more simple causal assumptions that we tend to make when formulating and implementing policies (Sterman, 2002). The dynamic effects of unanticipated and unrecognized feedback loops undermine policy goals, such as gender stereotyping (Figure 8) being reinforced rather than countered by diversity policy initiatives. Yet, in contrast to the repeated diagnosing and redesigning processes for effective policymaking depicted in Figure 2, many organizations continue with these long-common diversity efforts rather than assessing outcomes, diagnosing the favorable and unfavorable dynamics driving the outcomes, and revising their policies.

Since they are based on findings from social psychological studies, the policy-undermining dynamics depicted earlier cross-validate and explain the earlier-noted findings (Section 3) from longitudinal societal and organizational field studies – namely, that U.S. society and its organizations in general have failed to improve equity through commonly used diversity policies that rely on diversity awareness training and attempts to institute fair employment practices. In the following section, we examine social practices that undermine diversity policies, further limiting the success of existing diversity initiatives.

5 Policy-Undermining Dynamics Driven by Three Common Social Practices

The findings and models in Section 4 can inform organizational policymakers, work unit managers, and scholars how common diversity efforts produce unintended effects that are continually reproduced over time. To better understand and address these effects, they can draw on knowledge reviewed in this section on problematic social practices that spill over into organizations from the broader society. From research studies we identify three sets of anti-inclusive practices: *stereotyping and stigmatizing* different others; *making decisions based on implicit bias*; and *self-segregating*. These everyday social practices are often taken-for-granted and unconscious. They are a common part of human interactions, simplifying life and reducing cognitive strain, but in an organizational context they reduce the inclusion of underrepresented group members in productive work activities, hampering both equity and work unit performance. Table 4 describes the figures included in this section.

Regarding equity, a major insight is offered by the meta-analytic finding of subtle discrimination producing greater inequities than does overt discrimination (Jones et al., 2016). This finding points to the three inter-connected sets of anti-inclusive practices. First, with civil rights and legal compliance efforts over the past sixty years dampening overt acts of discrimination by motivating individuals to avoid acting racist and sexist, and to avoid believing that they are biased, subtle discrimination explains much of the continued employment discrimination as residing in implicit bias (Kurdi et al., 2019). Research reveals that nearly all individuals, regardless of their group identity, have largely unconscious social biases of one type or another, biases that they generally do not consciously acknowledge. Among dominant group members who are not consciously seeking to avoid their effects, implicit bias can produce inequitable personnel decisions through stereotyping and stigmatizing underrepresented group members. The issue is not whether we individuals of any group possess implicit biases or not but, rather, whether we succeed in controlling them.

Second, the finding on the strong effects of subtle discrimination is consistent with the widespread beliefs, discussed earlier and common even among some members of underrepresented groups, that our organizations are meritocratic and that there is a general absence of racism and sexism in society. Unbiased interpersonal behavior and conscious thought can mask implicit bias, enabling individuals to make inequitable decisions without realizing that they are doing so. This social process accords with the audit studies' findings (Section 3) on employment discrimination being a current reality and not decreasing over time (Bertrand & Duflo, 2017; Lippens et al., 2023). Inequities continuing due to

Table 4 Section 5 figures

Figure Number	Description
9–12	The complex, self-reinforcing dynamics of three everyday, ubiquitous, anti-inclusive practices of intergroup contact – self-segregating and interacting with discomfort, implicit bias, and stereotyping and stigmatizing – that shape unwelcome diversity interactions and inequitable decisions.
9	The three anti-inclusive practices operate in a self-prophesizing vicious cycle, reducing underrepresented group members' self-efficacy and performance by impeding interactions, collaboration, and knowledge sharing needed for high performance.
10	Self-segregating and interacting with discomfort by dominant group members self-reinforce over time, sustaining intergroup distancing and unfamiliarity. The resulting infrequent, superficial interactions produce inferior workgroup creativity and decision-making.
11	Triggered by prescriptive diversity initiatives, stereotyping and stigmatizing of underrepresented group members as incompetent and unlikeable reduces their self-efficacy and raises their anxieties, appearing to confirm the stereotypes.
12	Evaluators' personnel decisions influenced by implicit bias negatively impact underrepresented groups' compensation and promotion opportunities, lowering their performance motivation, increasing their quits and firings, and appearing to confirm stereotypes.
13	Combining the phenomena in the preceding models, processes among both dominant and underrepresented groups operate over time to sustain reduced inclusion, equity, and workgroup performance.

subconscious, subtle discriminating and stigmatizing (as in the form of micro-aggressions) accords with contemporary realities – namely, there appears to be societal progress on inhibiting the most overt behavioral manifestations of bias, such as sexual harassment, but discrimination continues because organizations fail to provide accountability for subtle stigmatizing and for managers' final personnel decisions driven by bias (Castilla, 2008, 2015). Implicit, subconscious bias also suggests the limitations of relying on legal sanctions that rest on decision-maker intentionality to discriminate.

Third, the restrictions and personal distaste for overt discrimination reinforces the natural human process of *self-segregating*. Individuals favor interacting with others similar to themselves (McPherson et al., 2001). Self-segregating, then, is the direct opposite of inclusion. The tendency to avoid differing others is further heightened by prescriptions on inappropriate intergroup behavior, with majority group members experiencing greater awkwardness and uncertainty in their interactions with underrepresented members, leading the former to interact superficially and infrequently with the latter. For underrepresented members, the desire to self-segregate is heightened by having experienced stigmatizing and discrimination in some of their interactions with majority group members.

The aforementioned phenomena are action-oriented. To emphasize their dynamic quality, we use the active terminology of self-segregat*ing*, stereotyp*ing* and stigmatiz*ing*, and mak*ing* decisions based on implicit bias. In our modeling of research-based evidence, these three categories of anti-inclusive social practices reinforce each other, combining to produce superficial and infrequent intergroup interactions (Bowman, 2013). As modeled in Figure 9, the lack of meaningful interactions inhibits the developing of familiarity, feeding back to sustain the three anti-inclusive practices.

The following figures break out the dynamic phenomena associated with the persistence and impact of each of the three anti-inclusive practices. Figure 10 models the evidence-based impacts of self-segregating and interacting with discomfort, delving into the negative consequences of such behaviors by the dominant group toward members of underrepresented groups. These behaviors result in infrequent and superficial interactions as opposed to inclusive, mission productive interactions. When self-segregating occurs, individuals remain unfamiliar with differing others, and underrepresented individuals are impacted by the continuing threat of being stereotyped and stigmatized, by inferior social networks, and by lack of knowledge transfer. This additionally impacts the workgroup's ability to perform due to inferior coordination, decision-making, and creativity.

Stereotyping and stigmatizing members of underrepresented groups (Figure 11), while societally produced and ubiquitous, reduces workgroup performance in organizations. Like self-segregating and interacting with discomfort, these practices impede working together and knowledge sharing. As presented in Section 4, stereotyping and stigmatizing are often triggered by organizational conditions, including prescriptive diversity initiatives and perceptions that underrepresented members are less competent. Stereotyping and stigmatizing lower dominant group members' assessments of the stereotyped groups. The results for stigmatized individuals are reduced performance evaluations, anxieties, lower self-efficacy

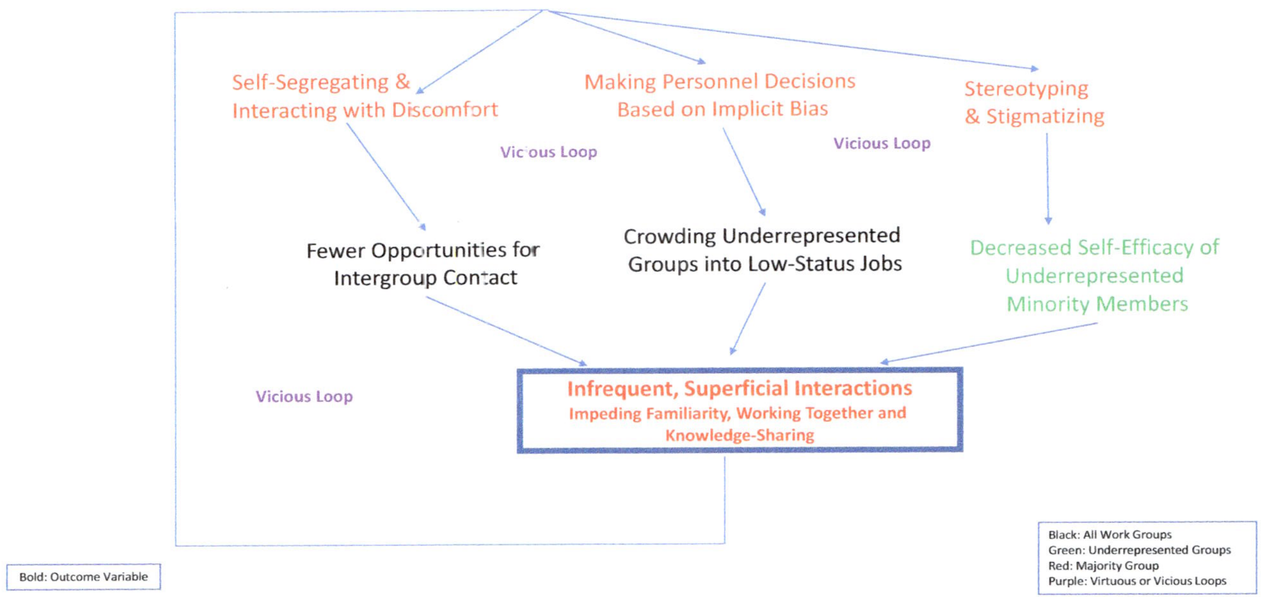

Figure 9 Three ubiquitous anti-inclusive practices of contemporary intergroup contact

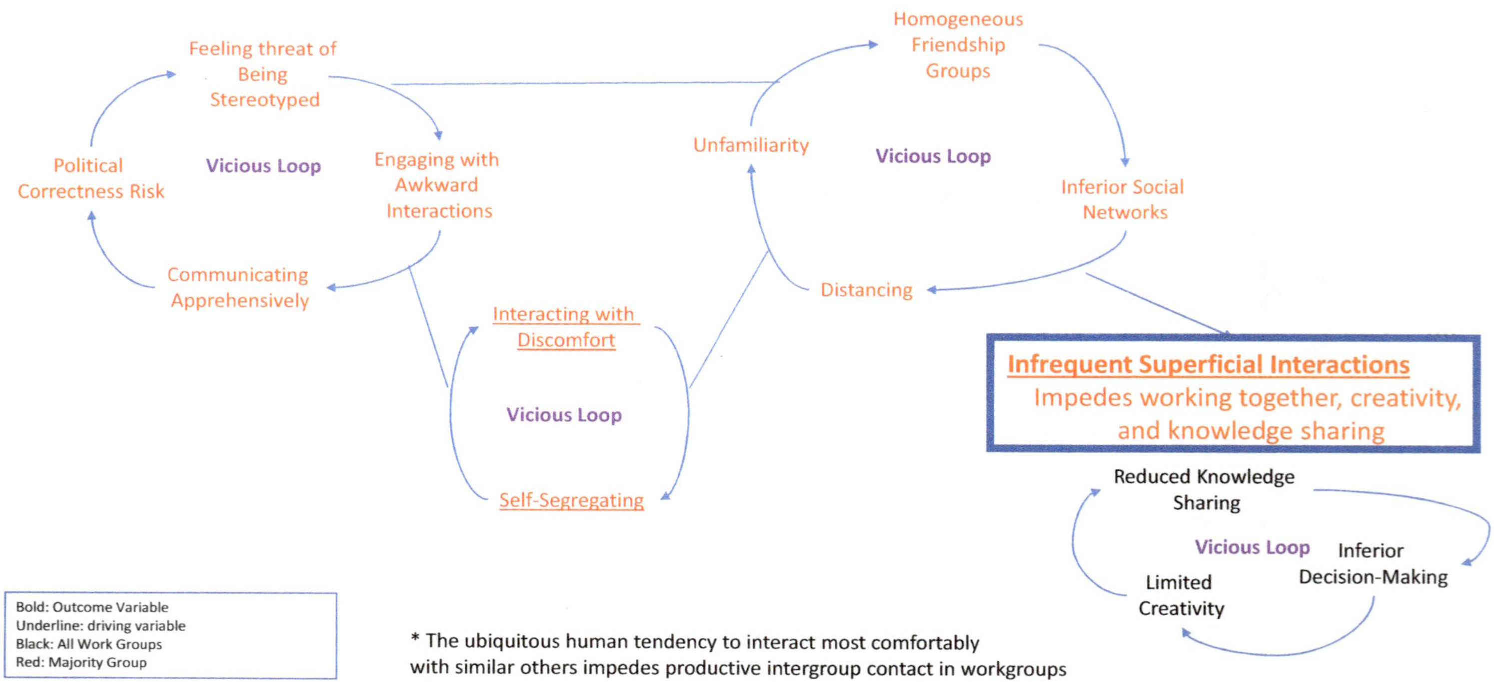

* The ubiquitous human tendency to interact most comfortably with similar others impedes productive intergroup contact in workgroups

Figure 10 Impacts of self-segregating and interacting with discomfort*

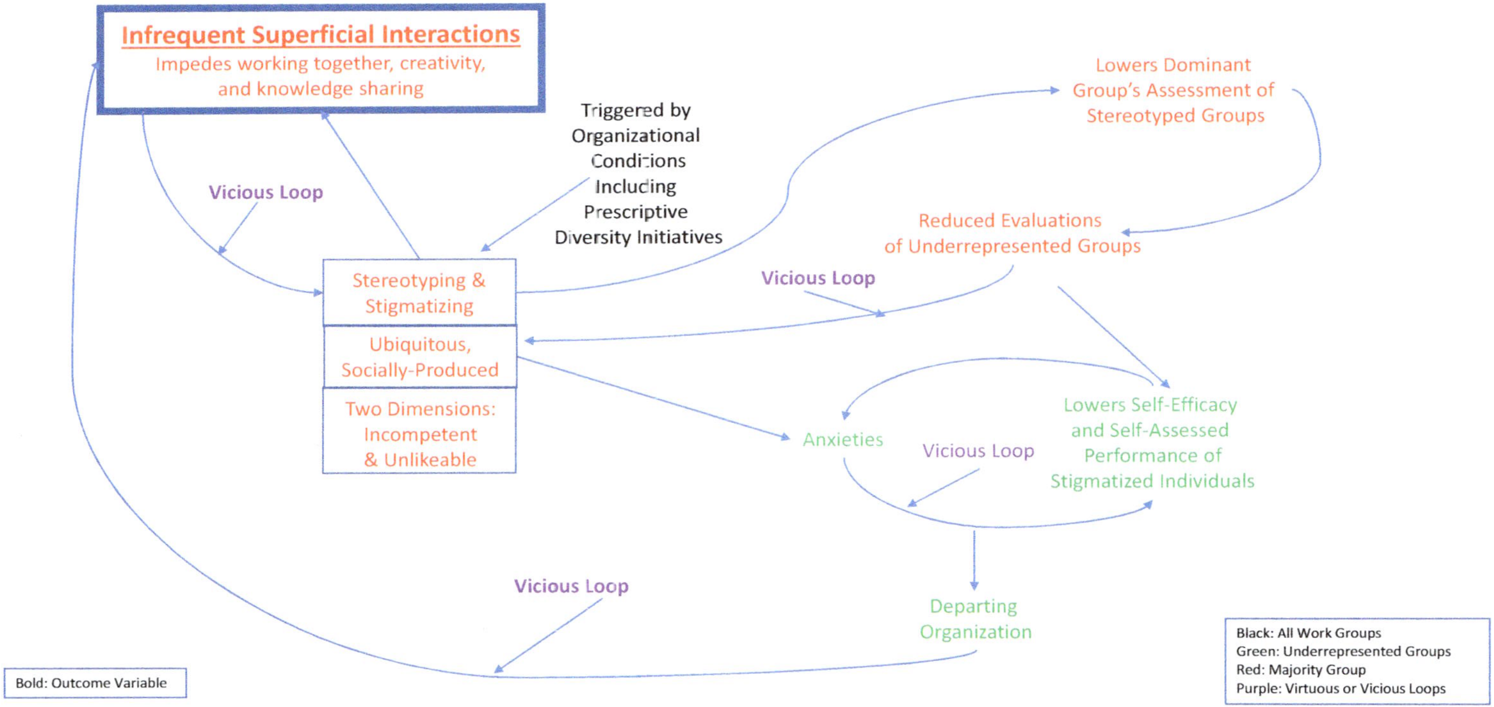

Figure 11 Dynamically sustained impacts of stereotyping and stigmatizing

and self-assessed performance (Leslie et al., 2014). These impacts reduce their incentives and expectations for advancing within the organization and create dissatisfaction that drives quitting the organization.

Making decisions based on implicit bias (Figure 12) is particularly insidious, since individuals do not recognize that bias is impacting their decisions about differing others (Kurdi et al., 2019). As noted earlier, the negative employment impacts of this subtle discrimination are yet stronger than those of overt discrimination (Jones et al., 2016). Controlling its effects in organizations requires targeted attention. Inequities and loss of performance occur when managers from dominant groups make biased personnel decisions resulting in negative outcomes such as reduced pay and limited developmental opportunities for underrepresented group members. Upset with inequitable rewards and opportunities, these members are more likely to have lower performance motivation and to depart the organization.

To summarize, the three anti-inclusive practices inhibit positively experienced, productive interactions and, through vicious loops, continually produce strong negative impacts over time on the workgroup, organization, and its members. Drawing on the models presented earlier, Figure 13 represents a simplified, but still complex, overview modeling of unintended effects and anti-inclusive practices undermining diversity policies. It portrays the myriad ways that the three anti-inclusive social practices reinforce negative behaviors, making sustainable inclusion difficult to achieve. On the left-hand side of the figure, dynamics involving the behavior and attitudes of managers and majority group members stymie the achieving of a set of diversity goals – principally, equity in development and rewards for individuals, and strong collective performance from a diverse workforce. These goals can be termed *sustainable inclusion*. The lack of productive inclusion, characterized by infrequent, superficial intergroup interactions, constrains work unit performance by hampering knowledge-sharing, coordination, and creativity. In addition, as modeled on the figure's right-hand side, the anti-inclusive practices affect the attitudes, performance, and decisions of underrepresented group members, further lowering sustainable inclusion and work unit performance. The net effects, then, include lower individual and workgroup performance, inequities, and departure of underrepresented group members from the organization, particularly the most qualified who have the best labor market alternatives.

The modeling of vicious dynamics in Sections 4 and 5, based on decades of empirical research findings, explains how organizational and societal progress on diversity has leveled off in recent decades and, for some groups, regressed. Combining what is known about the unintended, follow-on effects of current diversity efforts with findings on self-segregating, stereotyping

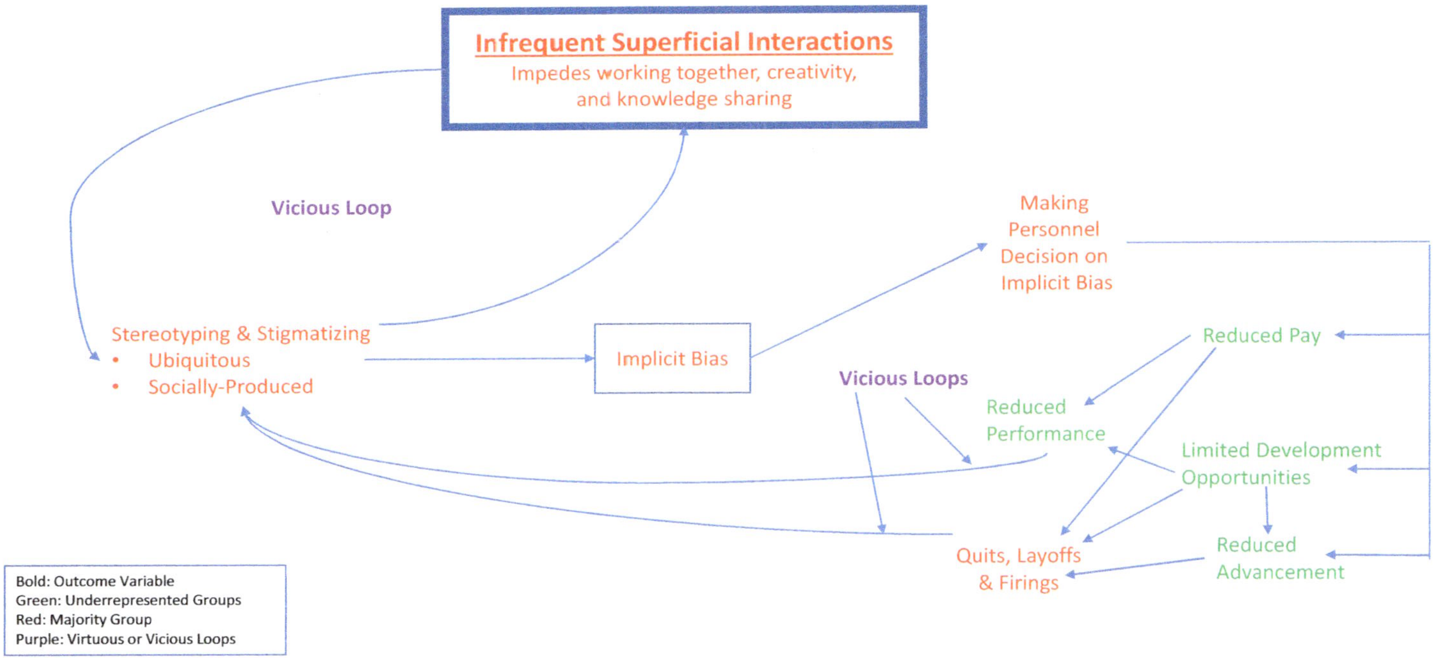

Figure 12 Stereotyping and discriminating sustained through implicit bias: Stereotyping and stigmatizing driving an unrecognized self-fulfilling prophecy through personnel decision-making

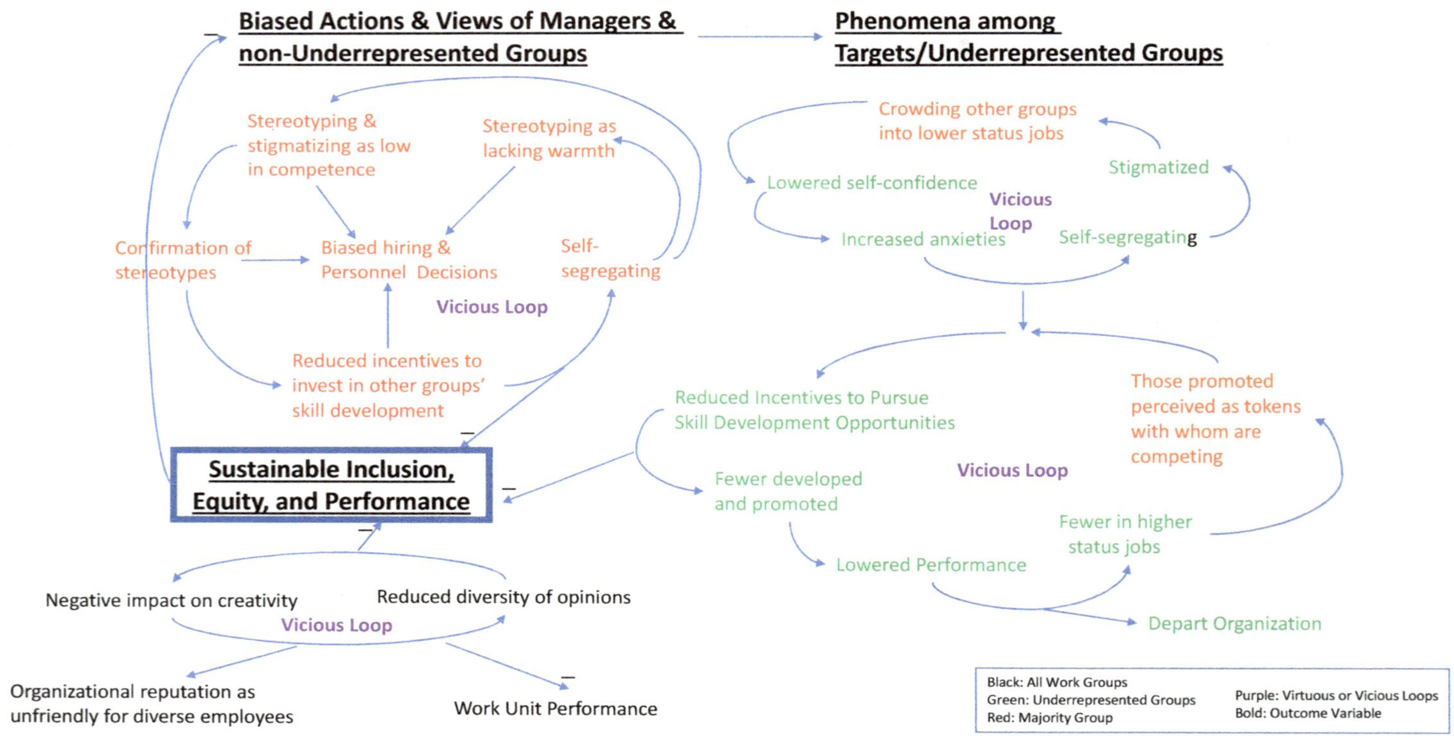

Figure 13 Negative impacts on the organization and its members: Reinforcing negative behavior

and stigmatizing, and making personnel decisions based on implicit bias strongly suggests that contemporary diversity management efforts will continue to *socially reproduce* (Bourdieu, 1977) a lack of inclusion and equity in organizations. The entire set of problematic phenomena is highly complex and continually evolving. However, some nonprofit and public organizations can and have addressed them successfully, achieving inclusion, equity, and mission attainment. To understand how they have done so, in the following sections we delve into the details of the framework for inclusive interactions, equity, and performance first introduced in Section 1, identifying leverage points for effective policy changes.

6 A Framework of Dynamics for Diversity Success: Identifying Leverage Points Based on Research Findings

The foregoing analyses point to a fundamental problem: the continued existence of prejudices – biases in the forms of negative stereotyping and implicit bias that are activated in self-segregating and stigmatizing behavior and in inequitable personnel decisions. Contemporary diversity policies have failed to deal effectively with prejudices. Those policies that identify and call out prejudices, such as mandatory diversity training, have fallen short on remedying them or, counter-intuitively, exacerbated them. This section's figures are summarized in Table 5.

Table 5 Section 6 figures

Figure Number	Description
14	Drawing on validated intergroup contact theory (Allport, 1954), intentionally structured diversity interactions positively reinforce adaptive practices and learning, increasing interpersonal comfort while decreasing prejudices and stigmatizing, leading to inclusion, equity, and performance.
15	Over time, managerially structured social practices for inclusion erode anti-inclusive practices by leading to adaptive learning among workgroup members.
16	An overarching framework for inclusive interactions, equity, and performance centers on four sets of inclusive practices – those for inclusive interactions, socialization, behavior accountability, and outcomes accountability. The reinforcing cycle created by the combination of these practices counters anti-inclusive practices and supports sustainable inclusion.

One body of research findings points to pathways for success with inclusion, equity, and work unit performance through a leverage point that does reduce prejudices, *intergroup contact*. Surprisingly, these findings have not influenced contemporary policies. Instead, the commonly attempted, but ineffective, leverage point for diversity policy is individuals' attitudes – hence, the reliance on training sessions to make members cognitively aware of bias and inappropriate behavior. The ineffective and even counter-effective impacts of mandatory training on the advancement outcomes of underrepresented groups (Dobbin et al., 2015; Kalev et al., 2006) is explained by several of the models presented earlier. Training is one among several policy efforts that send signals that many organizational members interpret in ways that sustain policy-undermining feedback loops, as detailed in Section 4. Diversity training attempts to change attitudes directly, but individuals tend to resist such attempts and to draw unintended interpretations from them.

A substantial, well-validated body of research points, instead, to the different and neglected leverage point of direct interpersonal interactions of differing individuals, termed *diversity interactions* (Bowman, 2013). As many of the models above indicate, those interactions, at the level of interpersonal *behavior*, frequently cause significant problems. For instance, stereotyping at the purely cognitive level – that is, attitudes – becomes problematic when it drives actual behavior, notably self-segregating, stigmatizing, and making biased personnel decisions. As modeled earlier, those behaviors affect the rewards, developmental opportunities, performance, and self-efficacy of underrepresented group individuals. One-time, mandatory awareness training aimed at attitudes has proven insufficient to change biased behavior, since such training leads, unintendedly, not only to sustaining bias but also to self-segregating and interacting superficially. With majority group individuals wary of behaving inappropriately and underrepresented group members concerned about being disrespected, both groups avoid diversity interactions when possible, foregoing opportunities to learn about each other and interact productively.

6.1 Intergroup Contact

Since they represent opportunities to learn how to behave productively with differing others, the quantity and quality of diversity interactions, of intergroup contact, are a key to achieving, or not, diversity policy goals. In contrast to the limitations of direct attitude change efforts, a long-standing body of social psychology research finds that changing individuals' behavior produces changes in attitudes. Through cognitive dissonance and over time, individuals tend to bring their attitudes in line with their actual behavior (Festinger, 1962).

Similar to cognitive dissonance, but more specific to diversity interactions, intergroup contact theory (Allport, 1954) posits that intergroup interactions produce reductions in prejudicial attitudes. Decades of research, analyzed in a continuing series of systematic literature reviews (Hewstone & Swart, 2011; Paluck et al., 2019; Pettigrew & Tropp, 2006) support the prejudice reduction effects, even when contact is experienced vicariously, as in reading a novel, or negatively, such as interacting with the homeless (Lee et al., 2004). However, the positive effects have been found to be stronger when contact occurs in the particular conditions identified by Allport, including having common goals and institutional support.

An overview of recent research reviews (Paolini et al., 2021) identifies further development of knowledge on intergroup contact: that the reduction of prejudices from contact with a member of one group generalizes to other members of that group and, further, to other groups; the value of contact-seeking, intimacy-building, and indirect contact (observing a member of one's own group interacting with a member of another group); and that challenges to prejudice reduction result from intergroup contact that is experienced negatively. The challenges of negative contact reside in two competing effects: first, some episodes of negative contact impede prejudice-reduction more than episodes of positive contact aid prejudice reduction, but, second, the frequency of contacts experienced positively is substantially greater than of those experienced negatively, even in seemingly unfavorable settings (Schafer et al., 2021). The implication is that, on average, enough contact will be experienced positively to overcome the less frequent negative experiences. These findings point to the importance of leaders creating workplace conditions in which contact is experienced positively, but leaders can err on the side of creating more rather than less contact.

We know, then, that positive effects are stronger under particular social conditions surrounding the contact, such as engaging in collaborative activities (Pettigrew & Tropp, 2006). The strongest and most persistent effects stem from high frequencies of positively experienced diversity interactions (Bowman, 2013). As shown in Figure 14, we model such intergroup contact as leading to processes for *adaptive behavior and learning*. That behavioral adaptation leads not only to attitude change and increased comfort in interactions but also to personal growth for individuals, enhancing cognitive functioning and skills such as leadership (Boin et al., 2021; Bowman, 2013). Such valuable contact in the correct conditions is self-reinforcing. From repeated contact individuals develop interpersonal comfort and reduce prejudices and stigmatizing, encouraging their future interactions to be yet more frequent and comfortable. These processes operate in virtuous loops producing positive inclusion and equity

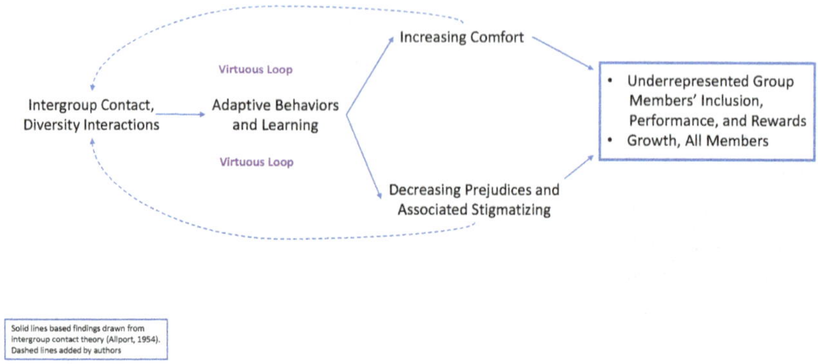

Figure 14 Positive processes for long-term improvement for underrepresented groups

outcomes over time for underrepresented group members and personal growth for all groups. Our framework (Section 1 and Section 6.3 below) models that such positive processes are driven by the structuring of habitual practices for inclusive diversity interactions, as we consider next.

6.2 Inclusive Interactions

Compared to diversity training's demonstrated limitations, the reduction of prejudices through productive intergroup contact offers organizations a highly practical leverage point – namely, shaping interpersonal behavior through *structuring workplace conditions* that cause interpersonal interactions among work unit members to be frequent and positive. Based on findings from intergroup contact research and our own case studies (Section 9), in Figure 15 we specify these conditions as being produced and sustained through managerially structured *practices for inclusive interactions*. Initiated and sustained by managers, these are social practices for inclusive interactions that work unit members follow habitually, bodily, and emotionally (Reckwitz, 2002), shaping their interpersonal contact to be frequent, inclusive, comfortable, and mission-productive.

Over time, with a delay, work unit members' positive experiences with their intergroup contact produces adaptive behavior and social learning, encouraging further intergroup interactions in a virtuous loop. Gradually, with a delay that our own research (Section 9) finds to be on the order of six or more months, this virtuous loop counters the anti-inclusive practices and infrequent, superficial interactions that undermine diversity policies.

Regarding such delays, all relationships depicted in the dynamic system figures operate with some degree of delay (Meadows, 2008). We note, explicitly

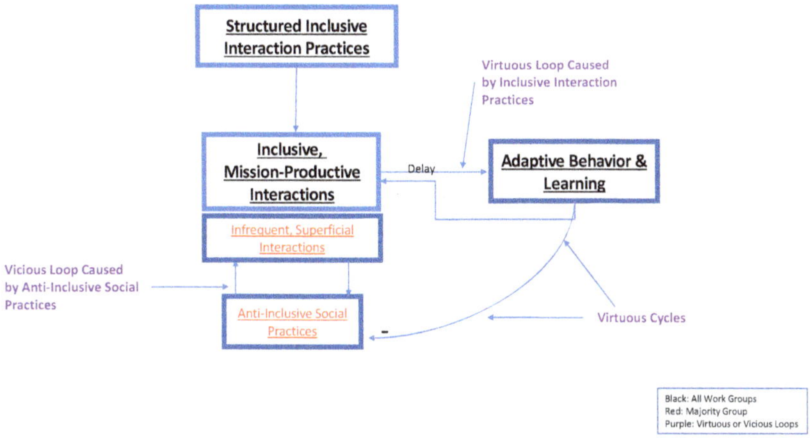

Figure 15 Virtuous and vicious cycles

in this figure and several others next, those delays that are most concerning for policy persistence and resistance. Delays in achieving beneficial effects can lead impersistent policymakers and managers to prematurely conclude that the policies are not effective and should be discontinued (Repenning & Sterman, 2002).

6.3 A Policy-Guiding Framework for Inclusion, Equity, and Performance

The overarching framework for inclusive interactions, equity, and performance (introduced in Section 1 and repeated here in Figure 16) brings together the analyses of the preceding sections. Proceeding from the systematically reviewed findings from bodies of research on intergroup contact carried out across the globe, inclusive mission-productive interactions are fostered through three sets of inclusive practices depicted across the top of the figure – *structured inclusive interaction practices, socialization practices, and behavior accountability practices* – and by a set of practices for *outcomes accountability*. These practices are detailed in Section 7, and their use in organizations is illustrated by cases in Section 9.

Each set of practices represents a leverage point. Those for inclusive interactions are labelled as the primary leverage point due to their often-neglected ability to reduce prejudices. The four leverage points best act in combination to reinforce each other. Their practices apply to all members and all interpersonal interactions, not only to diversity interactions, thereby finessing the negative effects created by signals associated with explicit, prescriptive diversity policies. By reducing prejudices, strategically combining the practices for

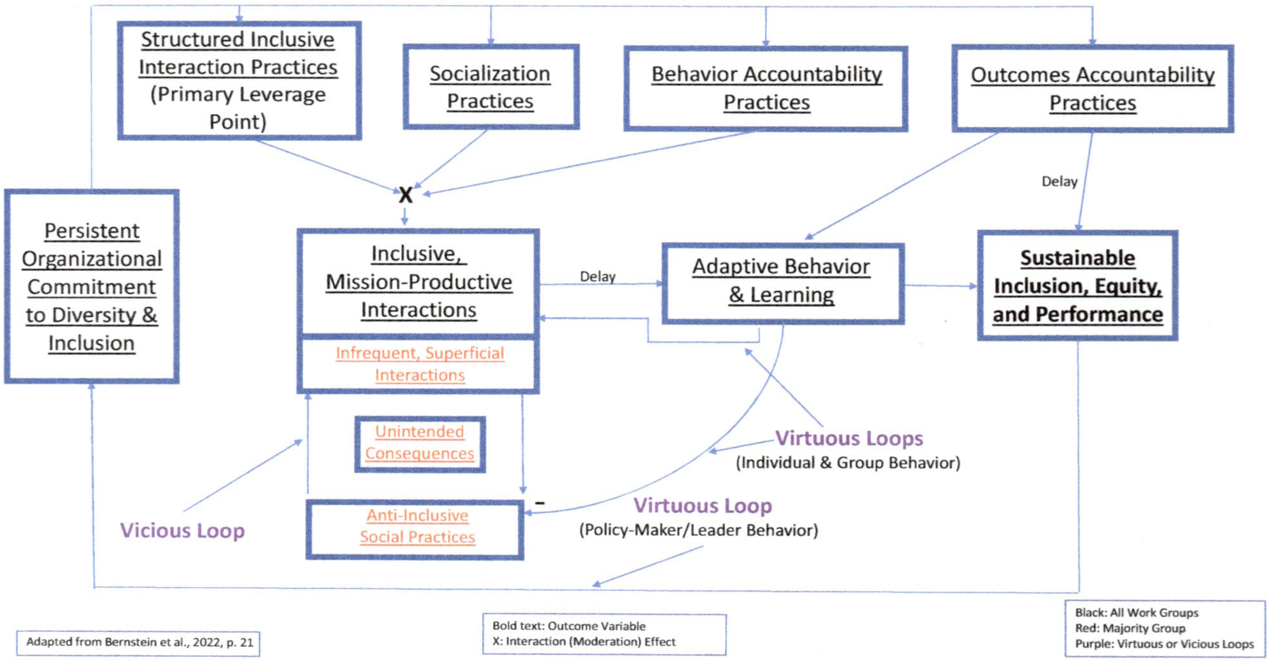

Figure 16 Framework for inclusive interactions, equity, and performance

inclusive interactions and socialization with the other two sets of practices depicted in the framework aids in mitigating the unintended and potentially undermining effects those latter two practices can otherwise produce.

Following the empirical findings on intergroup contact, adaptive behavior and learning occur when inclusive interactions prevail over time – that is, with a delay – by reducing prejudices (stereotyping and stigmatizing) and sustaining work-productive inclusion and equity. Once prejudices begin to be reduced meaningfully, the fourth leverage point – outcomes accountability practices that monitor and act on data reflecting inclusion and equity (Castilla, 2015) – can further aid in producing adaptive learning and improving equity in rewards.

To produce such results, a key point from system dynamics (Section 2, Figure 2) deserves emphasis: given the reality of delayed effects, if inclusive interaction practices and accountability practices are to prevail, leaders must be persistent in gathering feedback information on adaptive behavior, diagnosing and redesigning inclusive practices over time, and maintaining commitment until adaptive learning occurs in a sustained fashion. As adaptive learning begins to improve inclusion, equity, and mission attainment, leaders' commitment to the continued evolving of effective inclusive practices will be reinforced, completing a virtuous loop.

Next, Section 7, breaks out the inclusive practices depicted at the top of the framework, while the cases in Section 9 reveal the myriad forms that these practices can take, depending on an organization's mission and context.

7 Structuring Practices for Sustainable Inclusion

In this section elements of the framework are broken out in the form of dynamic models, treating in turn each of the leverage points – that is, the four sets of practices for inclusion and equity. Table 6 lists the figures for this section.

7.1 Structured Inclusive Interaction Practices

The large body of research on intergroup contact (Section 6) and our own research (Bernstein et al., 2022) point to intergroup contact being particularly effective in the presence of six habitual practices. These *inclusive interaction practices* can be structured by organizational leaders and managers. The practices are: (1) pursuing a shared task orientation or mission; (2) mixing members frequently and repeatedly; (3) collaborating with member interdependence; (4) handling conflict constructively; (5) exhibiting interpersonal comfort and self-efficacy; (6) and ensuring equal insider status for all members. We propose that these six represent a set of mutually reinforcing practices, complementing each

Table 6 Section 7 figures

Figure Number	Description
17	Virtuous cycles for sustained inclusion are driven by structuring six practices for inclusive interactions: shared task or mission; mixing members repeatedly and frequently; collaborating with member interdependence; handing conflict constructively; exhibiting interpersonal comfort and self-efficacy; and ensuring equal insider status.
18	Over time, structuring inclusive interaction practices produces positive, collaborative diversity interactions that sustain three virtuous cycles through: (a) improved interpersonal comfort increasing the frequency of interactions; (b) improved comfort leading to interpersonal self-disclosure and familiarity leading to reduced prejudices; and (c) enhanced interpersonal skills and higher mission attainment encouraging further diversity collaborations.
19	Formal socialization practices, particularly those for personal identity socialization, encourage the use of members' distinctive talents for mission attainment and facilitate informal interactions, friendship formation, trust-building, and retention of diverse members.
20	Being accountable for one's behaviors and those of the workgroup members supports behaving respectfully and resolving conflicts constructively, facilitating more comfortable and willing interactions.
21	Outcomes accountability practices, when combined with the other sets of inclusive practices and when in the form of a managerial task force, encourage the following of various fair employment practices for equitable personnel decisions.
22	Examining Al-Anon, the national organization that supports individuals with family or friends who are alcoholics, norms of behaviors and structured interaction practices enable acculturation of new members. Established rules guide appropriate behaviors and enable conflicts to be more easily resolved.
23	An organization may have diverse representation at the organizational level, yet fail to be diverse at the workgroup or team level. In the GSUSA, the girl membership as a whole and in particular councils can be diverse, but within troops the scouts and their leaders are mostly homogeneous. Inter-troop activities sometimes offer opportunities for interactions with diverse others, but do not occur frequently enough for sustained diversity interactions or adaptive learning.

other in a synergistic way to sustain meaningful, productive interpersonal behavior through a number of virtuous feedback loops.

To avoid the unintended, backlash effects of diversity-explicit policies, inclusive practices can be promoted by managers as means to improve mission performance through members engaging productively with each other. Combined with applying the inclusive interaction practices to all members, promoting them for superior mission attainment rather than as a diversity policy reduces the negative, undesirable reactions of unintended interpretations, heightened prejudices, and stereotype threat that follow from prescriptive diversity efforts. Instituting inclusive interaction practices that boost performance produces behavioral change toward members of underrepresented groups as stereotypes are challenged through repeated positive interactions and productive performance outcomes. The resulting reduction in prejudices and stereotype threat to underrepresented group members contributes to their performing well and being judged more positively by themselves and others, leading them to receive more equitable rewards. With such prejudice-reducing, equity-improving, and performance-enhancing effects, the six practices for inclusive interactions reinforce one another in a virtuous loop (Figure 17).

Engaging in the six inclusive interaction practices drives three virtuous reinforcing loops shown in Figure 18. As we found in a study of an on-campus voluntary organization with a mission of community service (see Section 9), the three virtuous loops (A, B, and C) center on building collaboration and familiarity among all workgroup members over time, reducing prejudicial attitudes and behavior and enhancing mission performance.

Loop A (green lines) sets up a virtuous loop with positive, collaborative diversity interactions and feeling comfortable in diversity interactions leading to more frequent interactions (less-self-segregating) and, therefore, to less awkward and more positive, collaborative diversity interactions in the future. Loop B (purple lines) also begins with positive, collaborative diversity interactions that foster comfort, encouraging workgroup members to engage in greater amounts of informal conversations with self-disclosure, a key phenomenon for prejudice reduction (Marinucci et al., 2021). Over time, the high-quality interactions increase the desire for more interactions and less self-segregating, leading to interpersonal, intergroup familiarity and prejudice reduction that results in more positive, collaborative diversity interactions, completing the virtuous loop. Loop C (yellow lines) illustrates how mission attainment and task performance success, increased comfort in diversity interactions, and increased development of interpersonal skills sustain positive, collaborative diversity interactions among the group members. The three virtuous loops, then, center on building collaboration

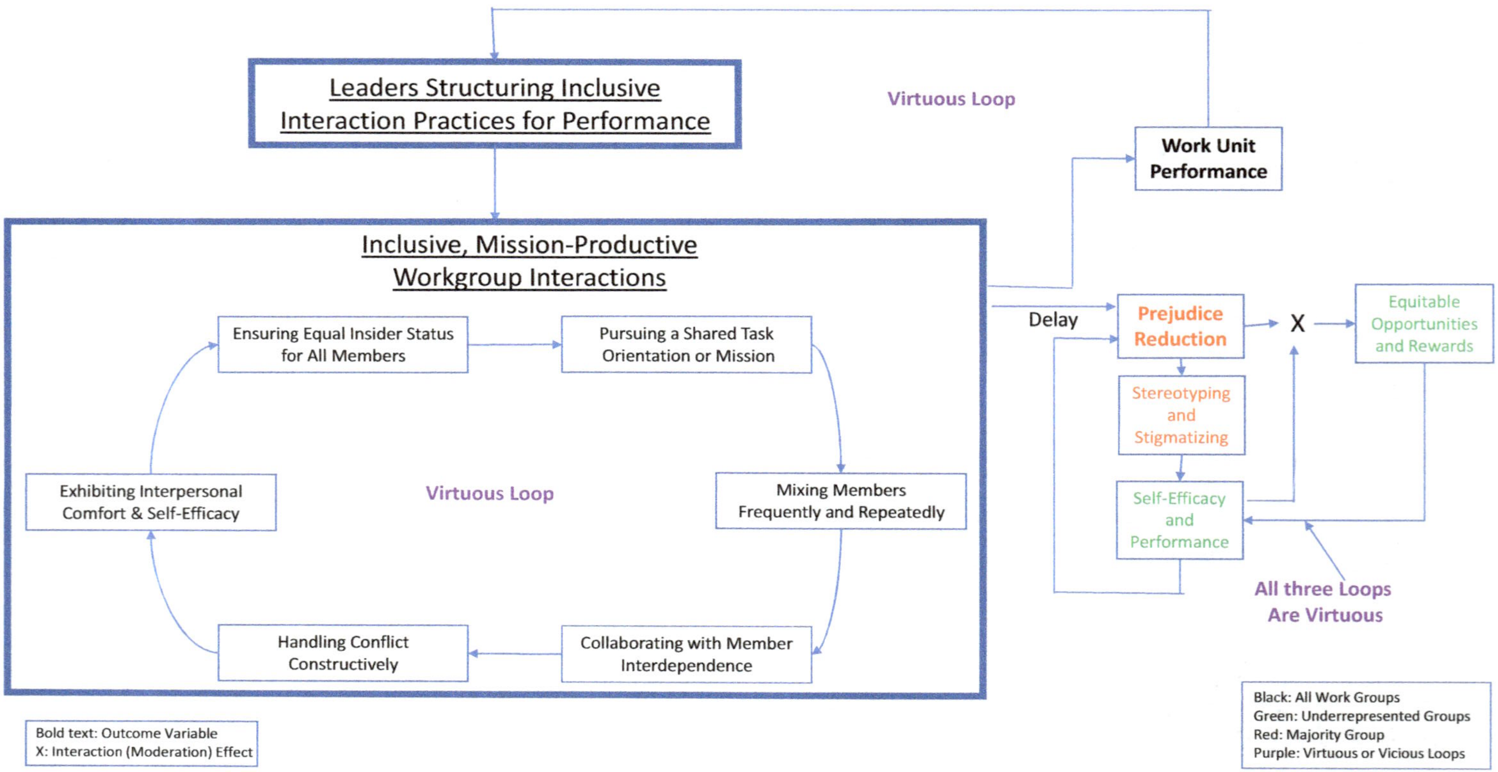

Figure 17 Structuring inclusive interaction practices

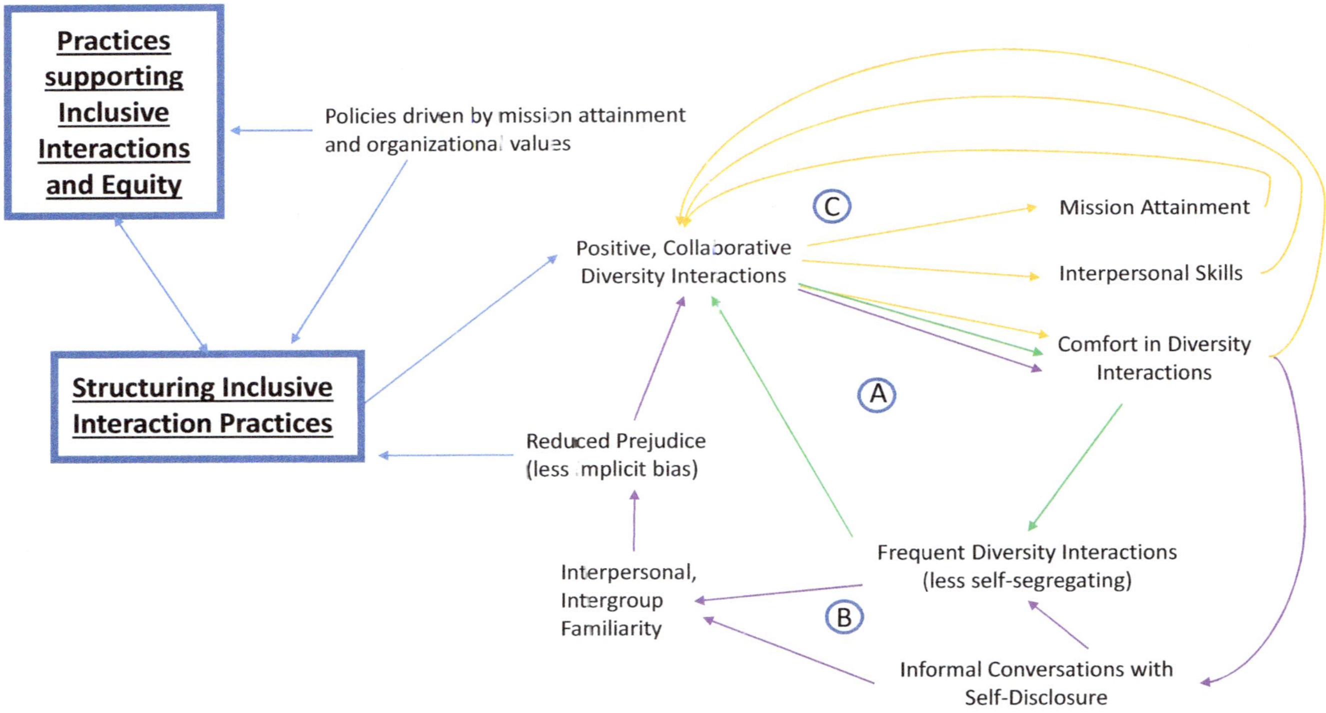

Figure 18 Virtuous loops building collaboration and familiarity

and familiarity among all workgroup members over time, reducing prejudicial attitudes and enhancing group performance.

Illustrating Meadows' (2008) point that paradigms are highly potent leverage points for creating favorable system functioning, the on-campus voluntary organization had developed its inclusive practices to fulfill its self-concept as a values-driven organization highly tuned to accomplish its mission. That paradigm attracted and sustained a diverse body of students and motivated them to follow its inclusive, mission-productive practices.

For the processes in Figure 18 to flourish as virtuous loops, we find in our case studies that managers and workgroup leaders achieve inclusion and equity using forms of inclusive interaction practices that are customized to their context and often, as in the campus-based, service fraternity, promoted by leaders without any reference to diversity. We model the effects of such well-aligned, customized practices in a fuller discussion of this service fraternity and several other cases in Section 9.

7.2 Socialization Practices

Figure 19 depicts the value of workgroup members engaging socially with comfort. Formal and informal socialization has been found to improve workgroup culture while increasing retention and performance (Bauer et al., 2007). As individuals participate in Socialization Practices, they build familiarity and trust that enables them to overcome interaction discomfort and the desire to self-segregate, thereby reducing the stereotyping and stigmatizing of unfamiliar others. One form of socialization – *personal identity socialization* (Cable et al., 2013) – is particularly relevant to inclusion. This form emphasizes individuating, seeing each person as an individual rather than only as a member of a particular demographic group. When new members are on-boarded, they are asked to identify the distinctive contributions that they bring to the group. For all the workgroup's members this individuating, performance-oriented process encourages interacting with each other for group productivity and seeing their fellow members for their talents, knowledge, and skills rather than for their gender and racial/ethnic characteristics. Personalized socialization links inclusion to performance.

7.3 Behavior Accountability Practices

These practices shape interpersonal behavior (Figure 20). They emphasize the importance of behaving respectfully toward one another, avoiding stigmatizing. The practices complement those for inclusive interactions and socialization and apply to all work unit interactions, not to diversity interactions only. Achieving

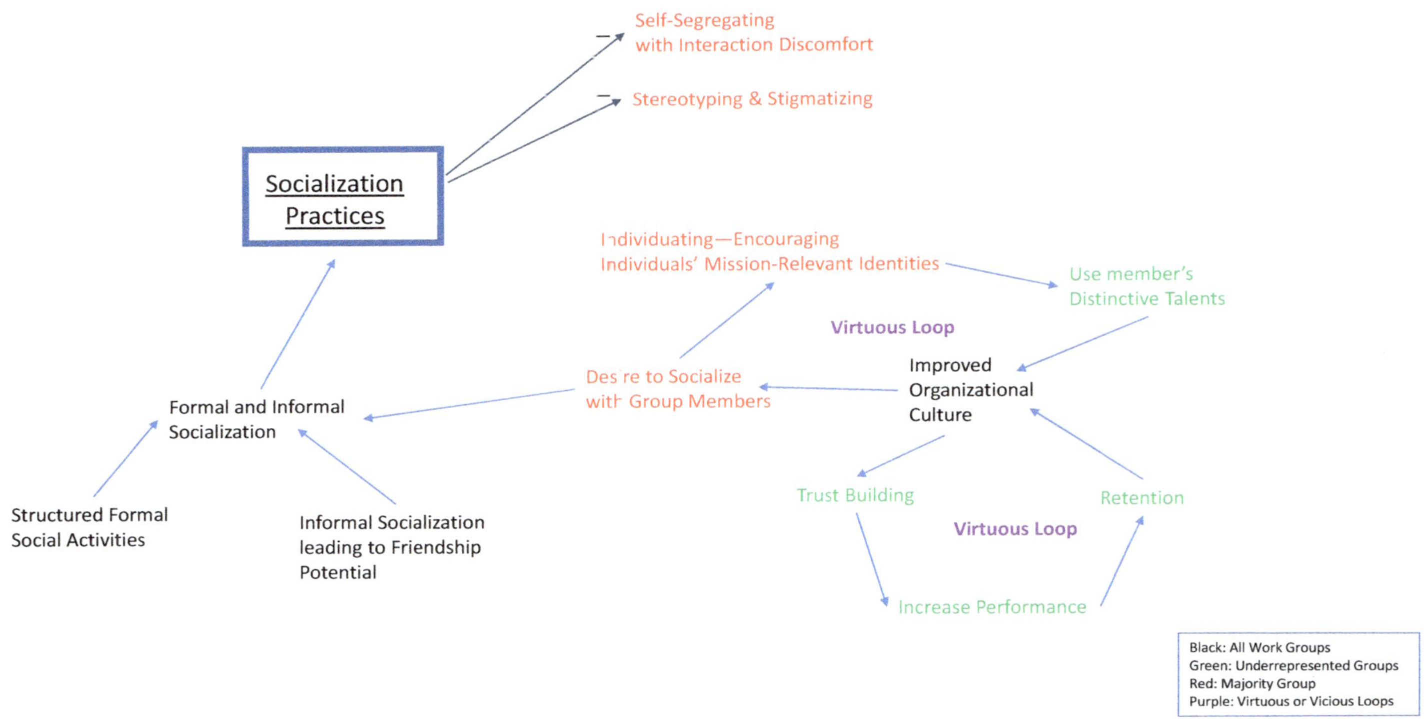

Figure 19 Socialization practices

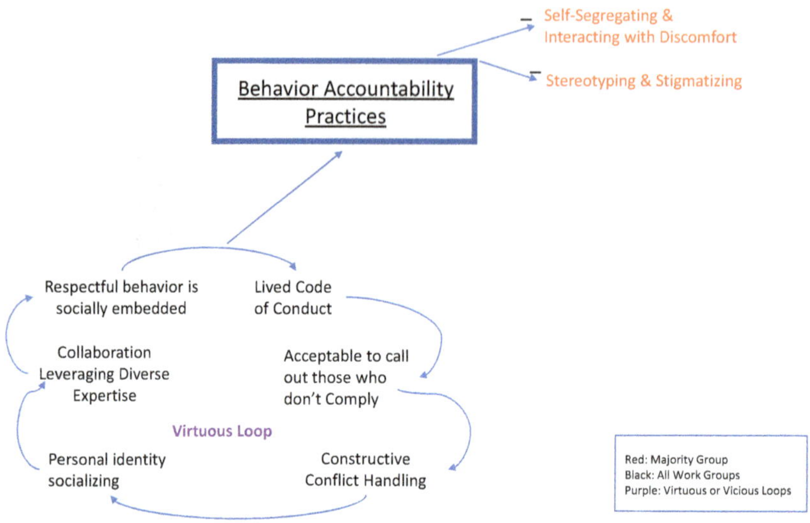

Figure 20 Behavior accountability practices

accountable behavior may require developing an explicit code of conduct to support practices for calling out those who do not comply and for constructively resolving conflicts. Over time, as individuals become accustomed to the socially embedded behaviors of the workgroup, of the organization's inclusive culture, they interact more comfortably and willingly. As stereotyping and stigmatizing are reduced, the work unit culture and performance outcomes are enhanced.

7.4 Outcomes Accountability Practices

Practices for outcomes accountability reflect two aspects of accountability. The first relates to personnel decisions and fair employment practices. The second refers to the ability of the work unit and/or organization to provide oversight to ensure that commitments to diversity initiatives are acted upon. Practices for holding decision-makers accountable for their personnel decisions (Figure 21) address equity for all organizational members. They include decision-makers using fair employment practices – procedures for recruitment, hiring, compensation, development opportunities, and fair appraisals. However, managers commonly have final discretion for making personnel decisions on pay, career development opportunities, and promotions, and typically, they lack accountability for those final decisions (Castilla, 2008). In the face of implicit bias affecting those decisions, managerial accountability is required to ensure equity. The challenge is overcoming "a systemic tendency on the part of human beings to avoid accountability for their own decisions" (Meadows, 2008, p. 157). This human tendency causes accountability system malfunctions,

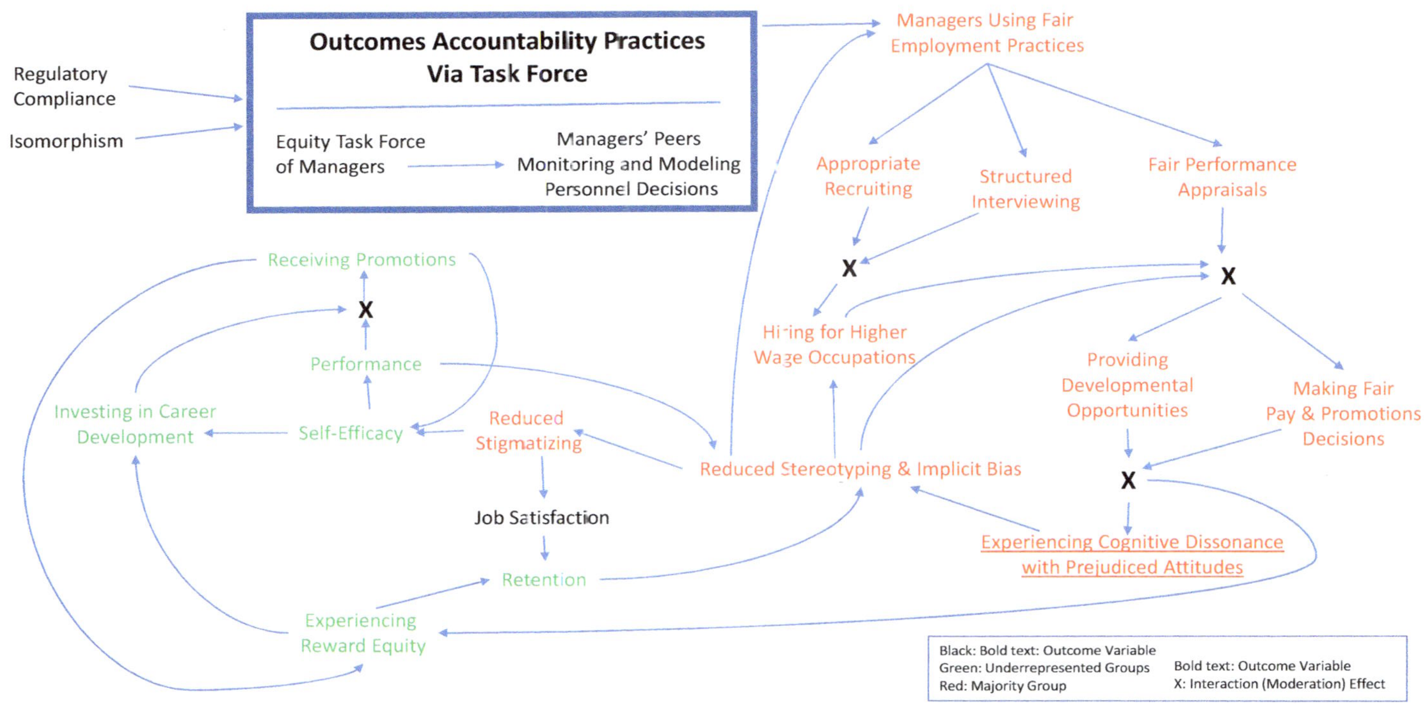

Figure 21 Outcomes accountability practices to counter stereotyping, Stigmatizing and biased personnel decisions

such as the unintended effects modeled earlier concerning members' reactions to explicit diversity policies. Consequently, as we discuss in the conclusions next, practices for outcomes accountability should be thoughtfully timed, designed and evolved to overcome such policy resistance.

Figure 21 conveys the complexity of processes associated with successful outcomes accountability. Many elements can be combined to sustain equitable personnel decisions and fair opportunities.

One evidence-based practice for outcomes accountability is assigning a task force of operating managers to monitor the personnel outcomes resulting from decisions made by themselves and their colleagues (Dobbin & Kalev, 2016). Initiating such accountability for final decisions is found to reduce, over several years' time, the pay gap for underrepresented group members (Castilla, 2015). Engaging task force members in behavior that pursues equity leads to reduced bias as their attitudes are brought into line with this behavior to avoid cognitive dissonance. Subsequently, as we found with a task force in a governmental science research unit discussed in Section 9, task force members model inclusive behaviors and attitudes that influence their peers. This type of task force is a highly feasible and powerful leverage point, one that has the potential to deal with the other sets of inclusive practices in addition to outcomes accountability.

The second aspect of outcomes accountability practices addresses the need for work unit and organizational oversight of diversity initiatives. While this may take many forms, as discussed in numerous cases presented in Section 9, having practices in place to ensure that inclusion and equity are maintained is vital. For example, as described in Section 9's cases, a board of directors created a standing board committee just for this purpose, while a service fraternity rotated leadership to ensure that their desired outcome of equity in leadership was maintained. As noted in Figures 16 and 33, delaying accountability practices may be wise, as some meaningful degree of prejudice reduction is a necessary first step to prevent backlash.

7.5 Sufficient and Insufficient Structuring of Inclusive Interactions

Two cases, depicted in Figures 22 and 23, illustrate the power of structuring inclusive interaction practices. In the first case, Al-Anon, information was obtained though open-ended interviews with organizational members (Bernstein et al., 2022). For the second case – that of the GSUSA, outlined briefly in Section 1 – in-depth interviews were conducted with GSUSA staff in two demographically diverse communities (Weisinger & Salipante, 2005, 2007).

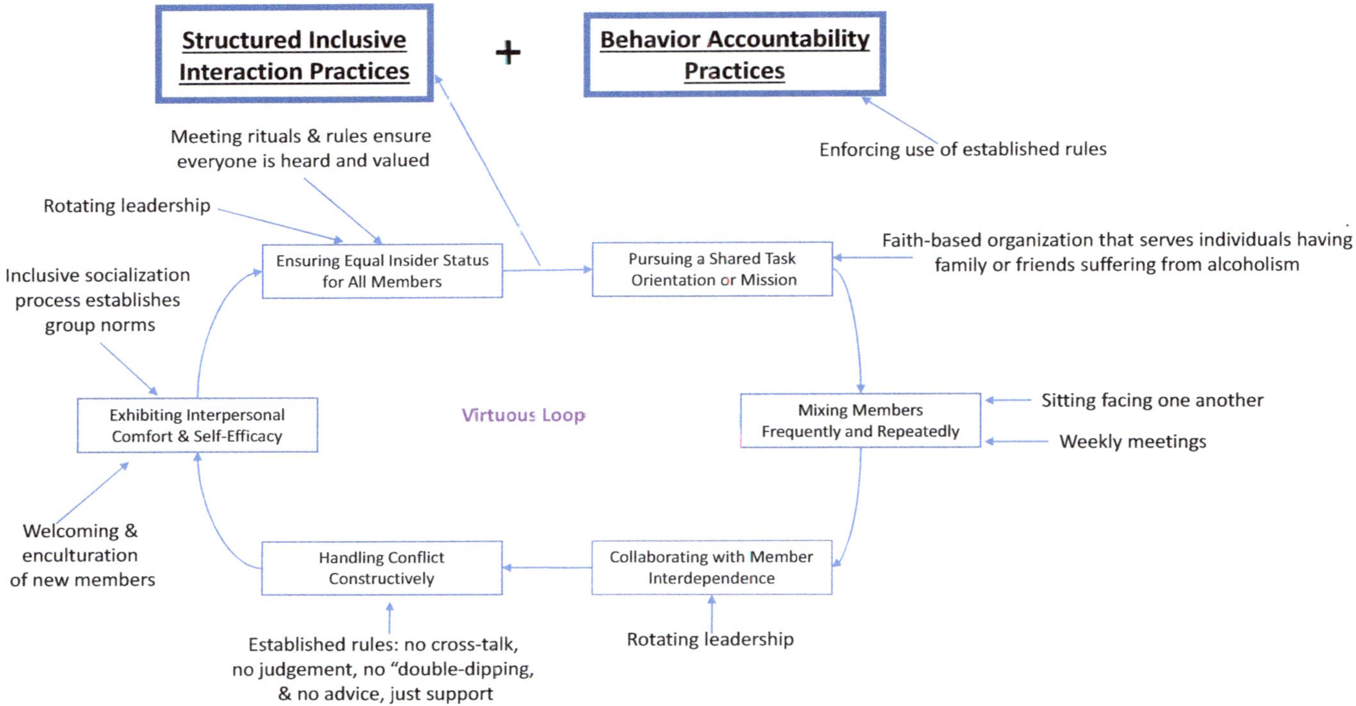

Figure 22 Al-Anon case

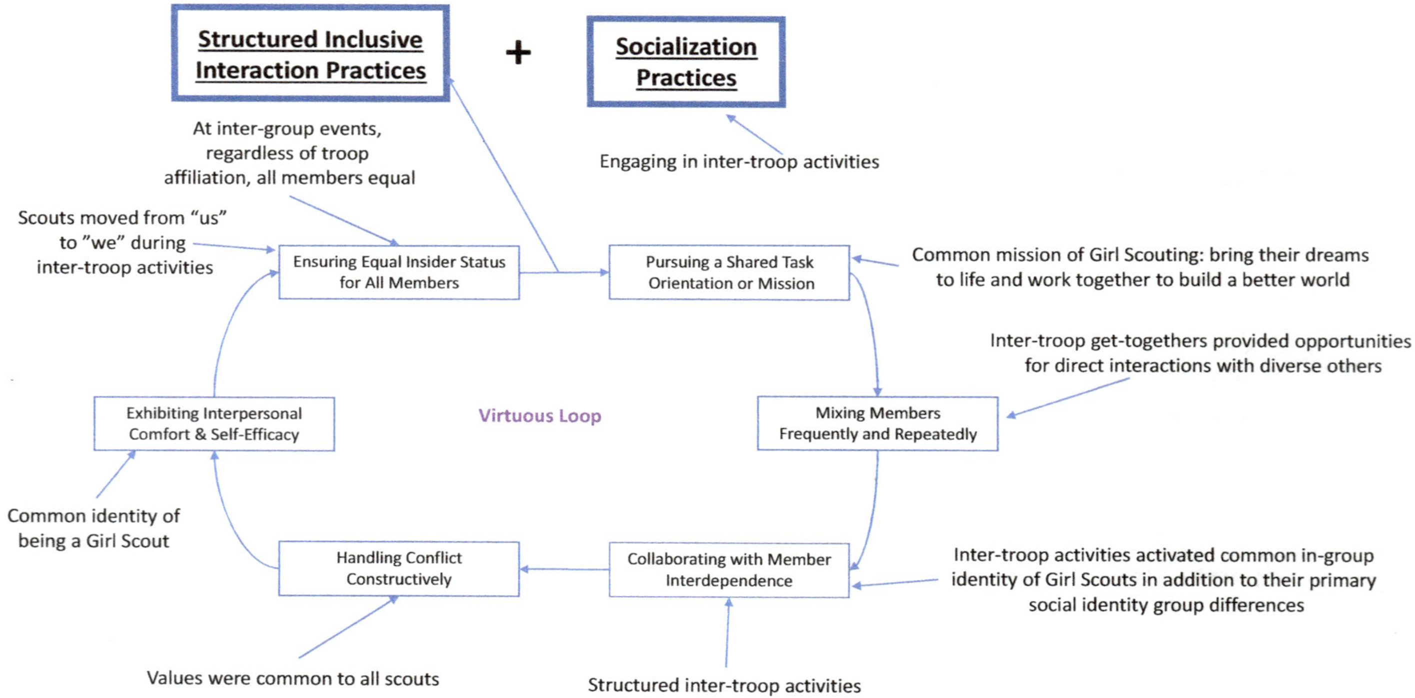

Figure 23 Intertroop activities, Girl Scouts of the USA case

Al-Anon is a widely recognized national faith-based organization that serves individuals having family or friends suffering from alcoholism; each of the structured interaction practices is utilized. Comprising small chapter meetings with diverse membership, Al-Anon welcomes everyone. The Al-Anon chapters have a set of rules that guide the meetings and enable conflict to be handled constructively. New members are quickly enculturated and accept the established rules. Because the organization's activities occur in the weekly meetings and each meeting follows the same format, the structured interaction practices are small in number, but they are effective in fostering the comfort needed for the members to share their stories and receive support. An Al-Anon member put it simply, "If only the whole world could act this way." The Al-Anon model, with its basic practices, illustrates the need for rules or norms of behaviors, acculturation of new members, and creating a comfortable environment.

In contrast, inclusion was often not achieved within the GSUSA. In keeping with a national goal of membership growth through increasing the diversity of its membership, during the 1990s the organization was among the first major U.S. nonprofits to pursue diversity seriously and persistently. At the national and regional levels, the organization succeeded in making its girl membership more representative of the population as a whole. However, individual troops tended to be primarily homogeneous, drawing the girls and leaders from their neighborhoods and schools. This was so even in stably integrated communities and schools due to common human practices of self-segregating.

In some GSUSA regional councils, intertroop activities provided opportunities to experience inclusion from direct interactions with girls in other troops of differing ethnicity, as modeled in Figure 23. During these intertroop get-togethers, the scouts engaged in structured interactions where all members had equal status, enabling them to, for a short period of time, forget their differences and move from "us" to "we." While some troops were able to engage in such structured inclusive interaction practices, the intertroop get-togethers were too infrequent for adaptive learning and sustained inclusion to develop. Another problem in some intertroop get-togethers was that the adult volunteer leaders of troops favored keeping their girls' activities within their troop, curtailing opportunities for experiencing differing others. The GSUSA case provides an example of an organization achieving diversity in terms of representation but, in most instances, not in terms of inclusion.

These two cases highlight the virtuous nature of the structured inclusive interaction practices. However, the GSUSA case demonstrates the need for all six of these practices to be in place and working together repeatedly over time. In the GSUSA example, because of self-segregating at the troop level and the lack of frequent diversity interactions at the intertroop level, stereotypes were not challenged and learning did not occur, resulting in a lack of sustained inclusion.

In Section 9, seven successful cases are presented. They are more comprehensive in nature, drawing on all four of the framework's practices – structured inclusive interaction, socialization, behavior accountability and outcomes accountability practices. But first, in Section 8, we emphasize the need for patience with respect to the timing of adaptive learning. As a result of the time it takes for individuals to repeatedly experience inclusive interactions and for stereotypes to be challenged, delays occur between the implementation of practices and the outcomes of sustainable inclusion, equity and performance. Failing to consider these delays may result in work units and organizations concluding that their diversity initiatives and policies are ineffective and discontinuing them.

8 Adaptive Learning and Its Timing

For success with diversity, adaptive learning is the key change process occurring over time, reducing prejudices by group members learning about, and from, one another. The system dynamics concept of a delay – that is, effects of an action being delayed for a period of time – is central to the processes of personal adaptation. This section's figure is summarized in Table 7.

From the overview framework earlier, we break out in Figure 24 the phenomena associated with adaptive learning. With a delay – that is, over time – as they follow practices for engaging inclusively and productively with each other, work unit members gradually learn behavioral skills for interacting with differing others. The learned skills mitigate awkwardness and superficiality to produce greater comfort, respect and satisfaction in diversity interactions. As the workgroup members engage in meaningful inclusive interactions over time, a virtuous loop develops. Members change their behaviors to comply with the various inclusive, productive practices. Their prejudices then gradually change

Table 7 Section 8 figures

Figure Number	Description
24	Adaptive learning occurs over time, with a delay, from engaging in repeated, positive, meaningful, inclusive interactions. Key components are familiarity and friendships producing reductions in prejudices, anxieties, and stigmatizing.

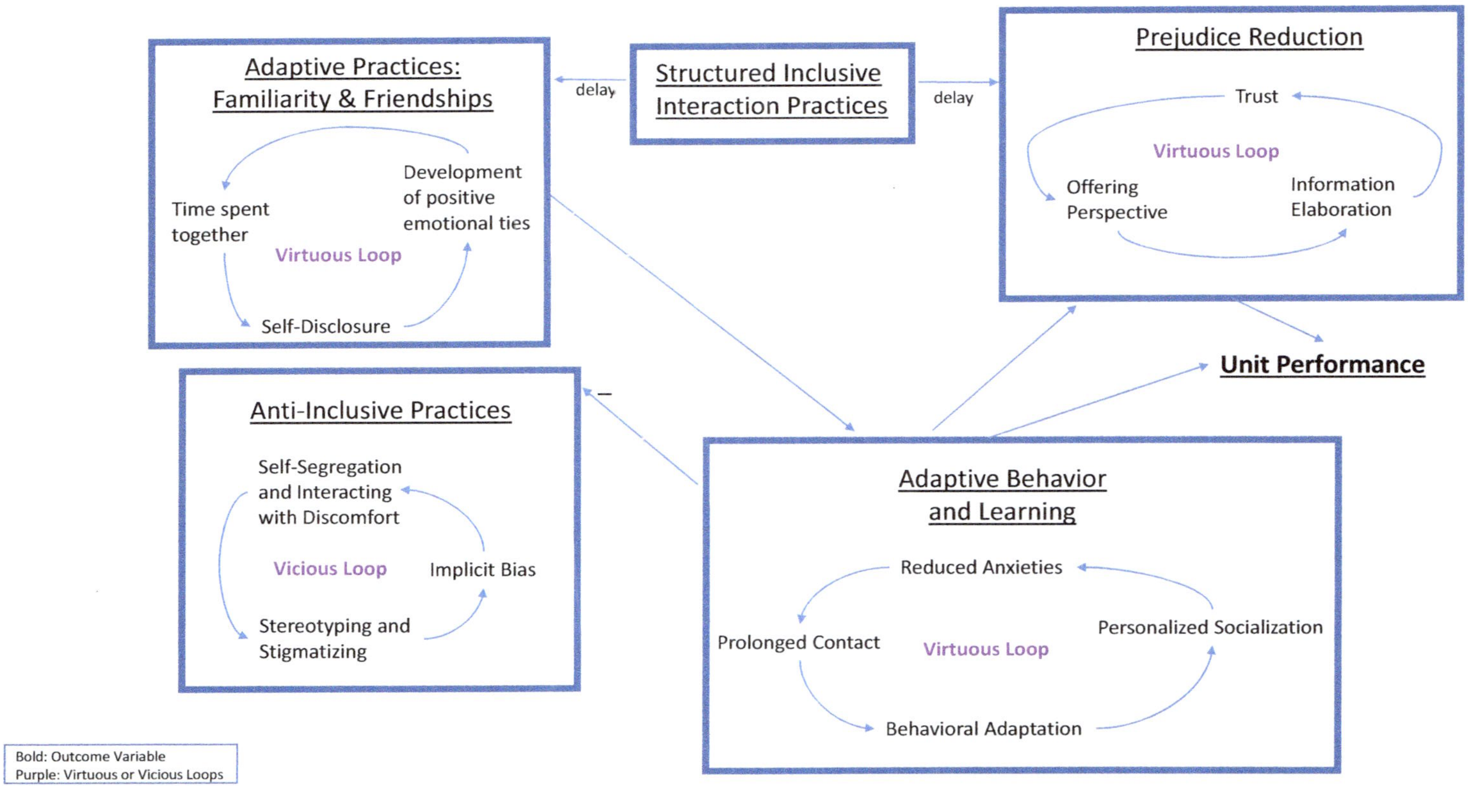

Figure 24 Adaptive practices, learning, and unit performance

as they bring their attitudes into line with their behavior. Members from all backgrounds are able to learn from one another as they collaborate and perform better as a group. Underrepresented group members, being included and respected rather than stigmatized, experience increased safety, self-efficacy, and trust in their colleagues. As the members learn from one another and become more comfortable interacting together, they are willing to interact more and continue to learn. This virtuous loop of adaptive learning contrasts with the vicious loop imported into the organization from the broader society wherein anti-inclusive practices produce infrequent, superficial interactions that further reduce inclusion and, ultimately, performance.

A delay exists with the timing of the relationship between the negative impact of the anti-inclusionary forces and the positive impact of adaptive learning. Based on findings from cases discussed in the next section, we realize the impact of the practices are not immediate. In the case of a governmental science unit, a tipping point occurred at approximately six months into a change effort aimed at improving interactions across functional groups. This case and several others revealed that approximately a half year of repeated interactions were needed for stereotypes to be challenged and attitudes to change meaningfully. This timing may be a minimum, since it occurred in organizations using a multitude of inclusive practices. Frequency and closeness of contact can be expected to govern this timing. Bowman's (2013) study of college students found change in attitudes occurred over the several years of college experience, but only among those students who experienced frequent, positive interactions.

Exactly what occurs during adaptation? Gradually, the adaptive practices of spending time together, self-disclosure, and developing positive emotional ties build on one another, supporting further inclusive interactions and adaptive learning in a virtuous loop. As a result, the anti-inclusive practices – self-segregating and interacting with discomfort, relying on implicit bias, and stereotyping and stigmatizing – are mitigated. A review of studies finds that intimate contact in the form of close, meaningful relationships leads to greater prejudice reduction, with workplaces being a context where long-term, close contact can be successfully structured (Marinucci et al., 2021).

As we found in our cases presented next, workgroup members' positive experiences in direct interactions reduce their interpersonal anxieties, leading to more personalized, meaningful, and prolonged interactions that are informal as well as formal. Members are increasingly willing to interact with other members of the group whom they initially perceived as different. Socialization practices and informal interactions lead to friendships with selected others, with familiarity increased through self-disclosure. This likelihood increases as the workgroup collectively follows adaptive processes – learned behavioral skills – that produce more positive emotions of greater respect and satisfaction, even when those interactions involve critiques and problem-solving (Ahmad & Barner-Rasmussen, 2019; Weisinger & Salipante, 2000). At the workgroup level, as trust is built, members are unafraid to offer their perspectives. More information and knowledge are shared, improving workgroup functioning for equity and performance.

The seven cases presented in the next section convey in detail the timing, feasibility, and efficacy of applying the inclusive practices found in the framework to produce adaptive learning and sustained inclusion.

9 Illustrative Cases: Achieving Successful Inclusion, Equity, and Performance

In this section we present from our research (Bernstein, et al., 2022; Bernstein & Aspin, 2024; Bernstein & Salipante, 2015, 2017) systems thinking models of organizational cases that illustrate the practicality of instituting performance-enhancing practices for inclusion and equity. For this research we focused primarily on interviewing people at organizations and work units that self-identified as "diverse, inclusive and equitable." We took this approach to delve into the practices that created positive, meaningful inclusive interactions. The interviews we conducted were lengthy and in-depth. We began by providing an overview of the framework followed by a set of questions focused on the realities within their organizations or groups with respect to the framework. Questions included problems and challenges that inhibit inclusion and equity from diversity, the existence of inclusion and equity practices that do and do not work, and actions taken that sustained inclusive interactions. When necessary, shorter follow-up interviews took place.

In Section 7, two cases were presented: Al-ANON and GSUSA. Both highlighted the significance of practices for inclusive interactions and the need for these practices to work together over time to foster meaningful, beneficial, inclusive interactions. The cases presented here are more comprehensive. The practices detailed in the figures come from the four sets of inclusive practices outlined earlier and provide insights on how various organizations elaborate their practices and customize them to their missions, task goals, and work unit characteristics. Evolving and operating dynamically over extended periods of time, the practices achieved inclusion and equity. As a set, the cases offer a multitude of forms that the practices can take. These various forms are available for selection and use in a range of nonprofit and public sector organizations. Readers will note that actions designed to fulfill one practice may fulfill others as well.

Table 8 presents a short description of each case. Fuller descriptions and figures that model the practices in each case then follow. All cases are from the

Table 8 Section 9 figure and case descriptions

Figure Number	Case Title	Case Description
25	Medical Research Unit	A medical research unit located at an elite nonprofit US medical center and composed of two knowledge-differentiated groups (pre– and post–medical school graduates), achieved its mission to be among the world's leading clinical research sites. Inclusive social practices result from the specific actions taken by the unit's director to create highly functioning and performing workgroups. The director instituted routinized practices to create an inclusive culture that was driven by the mission, collaboration, and the expectation of members treating each other, and their research clients, respectfully and fairly. Utilizing all of the framework's practices, the unit achieved sustainable inclusion, extraordinary levels of performance, and personal benefits for all members.
26	Service Fraternity	This, extracurricular, voluntary service, co-ed fraternity engaged thousands of students in community projects. Operating on hundreds of U.S. college campuses, its mission is Service, Leadership and Fellowship. Without explicit intention, it achieved diversity, prejudice reduction, and equity by following practices driven by its mission and values. Structured inclusive interactions, socialization and behavior accountability practices worked together to create a welcoming, inclusive culture that was fun and rewarding, motivating a diverse group of students to join and work together to help their communities.
27	Cross-Functional, Science Unit	In a governmental scientific research facility, employees had become siloed into their functional areas of administration, operations, and science research. The elite scientists (predominately White men), were unknowingly wielding their power in ways

Table 8 (cont.)

Figure Number	Case Title	Case Description
		creating an unpleasant work environment for the other two groups – administration and operations (mostly women and minorities). Internal consultants proposed to management a task force to improve unit performance. Over a period of 1–2 years and through intentional application of practices for inclusion, the task force members and their functional unit coworkers were able to confront underlying issues such as power dynamics and racism.
28	Leadership Fellowship	A leadership fellowship, sponsored by a nonprofit foundation, prepares people from underrepresented groups for future community engagement and leadership. At the beginning of each 18-month program the 13-member cohort generated "community agreements" to guide their interactions and behaviors, resolving conflicts and holding themselves and each other accountable. Employing all four sets of inclusive practices, the cohort, over about six months, built interpersonal trust, enabling them subsequently to speak authentically about such issues as race and experience adaptive learning.
29	Board of Directors	Nonprofit organizations, which frequently serve underrepresented groups, are in a prime position to model the advantages of diversity, equity and inclusion. Boards of directors of nonprofit organizations require inclusive practices to assure high performance from diverse membership. Effective efforts include representation on the board that mirrors client and community populations, and engaging in inclusive interactions to leverage the differing expertise of their members. Board bylaws and norms are ways to capture the practices outlined in the framework for inclusive interactions, equity and performance.

Table 8 (cont.)

Figure Number	Case Title	Case Description
30	Public Media Board of Directors	Driven by the employees, a public media organization's board of directors were pressured to diversify as a means to be more representative of their client demographics. Employing a consulting firm, the board created a strategic document making diversity, inclusion and equity central to board operations. A standing board committee was created to provide commitment to, and accountability for, the DEI strategic plan and ensure lasting impact on board and organizational performance.
31	Military Base	Initiated by a new Commanding Officer and using a top-down approach, a graphic strategic framework designed to reduce existing conflict and prejudices was developed for a military base with thousands of diverse military and civilian employees. Practices were guided by organizational values of integrity, teamwork, ingenuity, excellence, and service. As supervisors were trained on the strategic framework, culture and performance improved, one workgroup and team at a time.

nonprofit and public sectors. Organizations in these sectors are particularly amenable to the practices in the framework for inclusive interactions, equity, and performance because their members tend to share a mission- and values-driven focus. This focus encourages collaborative interpersonal behavior to accomplish the mission.

The variety of forms that the practices take in these cases is due to organizations having differing missions and contexts. For instance, some public sector organizations differ from nonprofits by having a legal mandate to be diverse. In both the nonprofit and public sector cases here we find the drive for diversity, equity and inclusion may be either top-down or bottom-up. However, many nonprofit organizations are likely to be less concerned with legal compliance and more motivated by the arguments for diversity outlined in Section 1 – moral/social justice, economic, client, and results.

9.1 Mission and Values-Driven Cases

We begin with four mission and values-driven cases. Each draws from a different nonprofit or public organization with a strong focus on mission achievement. Two – Medical Research Unit and Cross-Functional Science Unit – have employees and desired to be diverse in ways that improved their performance outcomes. The other two cases – Service Fraternity and Leadership Fellowship – are volunteer-driven organizations applying a values-driven set of practices. The cases illustrate the power of adopting elaborated sets of inclusive practices to drive mission attainment.

Figure 25 models the research unit performing and publishing clinical research in an elite nonprofit medical facility. Note in the figure the specific and multiple ways that each of the six practices for inclusive interactions and for socialization was reinforced. The director of the unit structured these practices in several, mutually reinforcing forms that were customized to fit the unit's specific context. To mention just a few of the depicted practices, a strong mutual goal focus was reinforced by the director regularly asking unit members to recite the unit's mission, ensuring that the mission was embedded in all layers of the unit. Collaboration and socialization were facilitated by the director when he insisted that the unit's facility design had offices with glass doors and a kitchen with an eating space for lunches and meetings. These physical features supported frequent and repeated informal mixing of the unit members. The director further stressed an expectation of fair treatment beginning with new-member on-boarding. Another example is the acculturation of new members by the existing members as opposed to an expectation that new members assimilate themselves into the unit.

The unit had three subunits of members: post-docs who had completed medical school; recent college graduates preparing for application to medical schools; and statisticians. The first two groups were transient and at particular points in their hoped-for medical careers. For all three groups inclusion and superior mission-achievement had personal pay-offs, advancing their professional careers by gaining skills and being associated with a highly performing unit. For example, over the years of the unit's existence 100 percent of the college graduate members were subsequently admitted to medical school. This is an example of outcomes accountability, along with the unit having the highest rate of publication of any similar research unit worldwide and productive interactions with patients and medical personnel. The mutual win-win situation among the unit's members helped to sustain its inclusive practices.

The medical research unit demonstrates Meadows' (2008) concept of self-organization, the power of a manager and workgroup members to initiate, add,

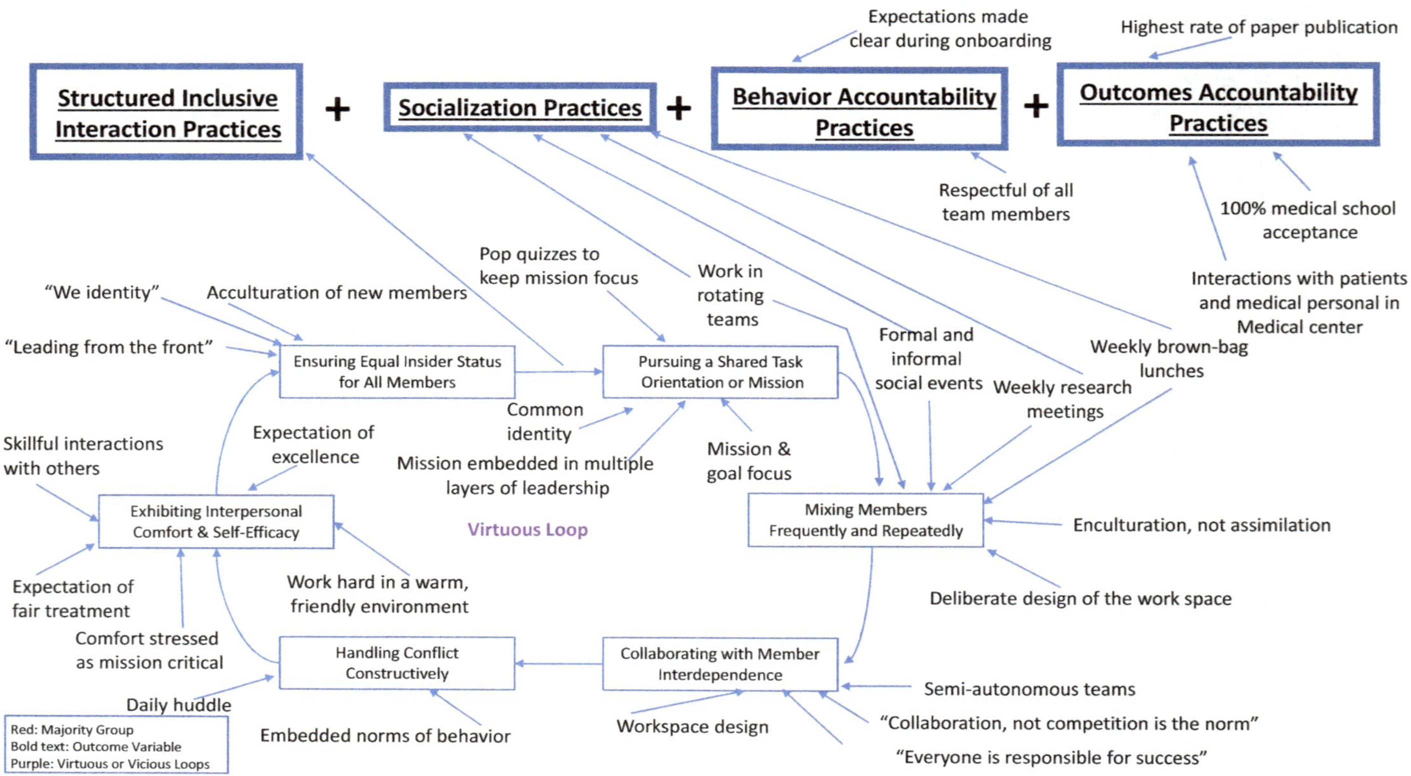

Figure 25 Medical research unit vase

change and evolve interaction practices. They were able to create new structures and behaviors that did not need to conform to those common elsewhere in the healthcare organization. Such performance-enhancing self-organization involves changing any aspect of a system, including virtuous and vicious loops and new social interaction rules. The ability to self-organize is the strongest form of resilience. In contrast, insistence on a single, static culture shuts down learning and inhibits resilience. For an organization's top leaders, the relevant leverage point here is encouraging variability and experimentation across work units to achieve productive, inclusive organizing.

Figure 26 examines how a co-ed service fraternity operating on many U.S. college campuses sustains inclusion and equity. Note that the specific forms of the inclusive practices differ from those of the medical research unit, to fit with the organization's college-based setting and mission. The service fraternity emphasizes three goals – service, leadership, and fellowship – but it is the mission of performing volunteer community service that attracts members, creates a common identity among them, and produces a workplace setting unlike purely social fraternities and sororities elsewhere on campus. As new members join, they are socialized and "forced" in a friendly way to interact with all other members frequently and repeatedly through structured fellowship activities, weekly organizational meetings where members sit in a circle to discourage clique formation, and the requirement for new members to interview all existing members. Mixing and collaboration occur when members show up to work on service projects, not knowing who they will be partnered with, and when they work on large annual projects such as the American Cancer Society's Relay for Life. Rotating leadership positions ensures equal status for all members, and the expectation of living the value of fellowship through familiarity, self-disclosure, and respect for one another leads to interpersonal comfort and self-efficacy.

The organization's inclusive interaction practices fit our general categorization but, as in the medical research unit, they have been customized to the organization's goals. Its inclusive practices explain why this service fraternity was singled out by campus administrators as a place where diverse individuals interacted well together, leading to cross-ethnic and cross-cultural friendships which were otherwise often limited on their campuses. The national organization was surprised to learn of this diversity impact since the inclusive interaction practices of its chapters were not pursued for diversity purposes but, rather, for its mission of service and its core values of fellowship. In this case, we see the overlap of practices. For example, rotating leadership positions to ensure equal insider status for all members is both a structured inclusive interaction practice and an outcomes accountability practice.

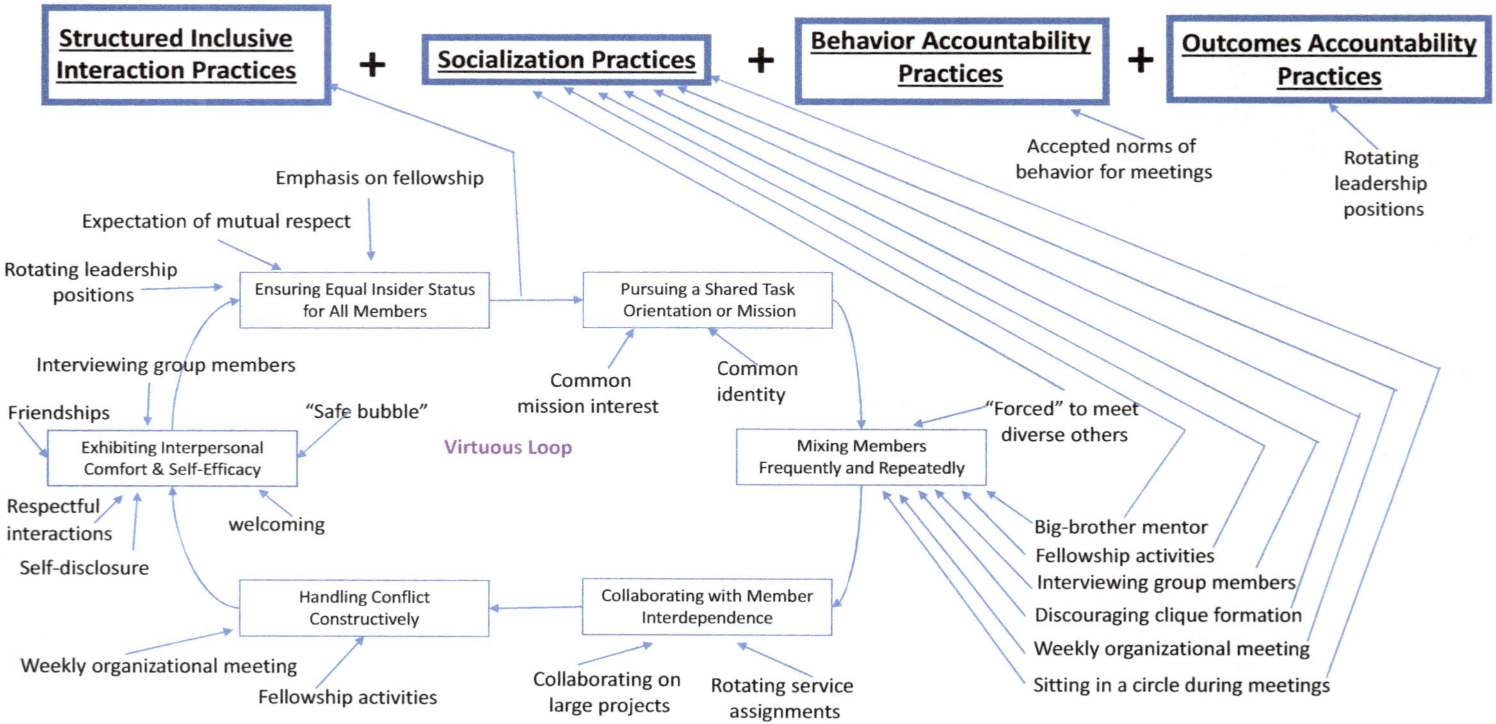

Figure 26 Service fraternity case

A third case, Figure 27, highlights a governmental unit, a scientific research facility in which a cross-functional task force was formed to address conflict among three employee groups – scientists, administrators, and operations staff. For the group facilitator who convened the task force, its purpose was to address inequities, poor work culture, and high-turnover due to power differences, as each group operated within their "functional boxes." Scientists were predominantly White men, with the other two groups composed primarily of minorities and women. The desire for the task force was driven by mid-level staff. The project was not sanctioned as a diversity effort. It was only sanctioned by top administrators when sufficient data was collected to demonstrate that the task force would improve unit performance.

Over the course of a year the task force members found that they engaged in the six structured inclusive interaction practices. They began with the task of creating performance enhancing models by examining how the three functional areas could work better together. By intentionally applying within the task force structured practices for inclusion, its members became able, gradually, to confront underlying issues such as power dynamics and racism. Structured conversations and guest facilitators enabled members to form a sense of community, engage in "good generative dialogue" and share lived experiences. Ultimately, the task force members became comfortable working together with the scientists who became more supportive of the two other functional groups, even advocating on their behalf to their superiors. Increased recognition of individuals' talents led to opportunities for transfers, development, and promotions. Members of the task force involved others in their functional areas, enabling its impact to spread throughout the functional groups.

Success was not immediate but, rather, developed over time. Meaningful change began to emerge after approximately six months, due to initiating and gradual following numerous practices for inclusion. This case highlights policy persistence – the task force leaders and members paid attention to issues that arose as they proceeded. As a result, there was an *elaboration* of effective practices over time, with the practices complementing each other. Having task force leaders and support staff attuned to watching for successes and challenges was a demonstrated advantage in producing project success.

Figure 27 illustrates the many practices used by the task force. As depicted in the figure, over time beneficial interplay occurred between the structured practices for inclusive interactions and those for socialization, behavior accountability, and outcomes accountability. Adaptive learning developed and was sustained, the changes being reported to have remained in place years after the dissolution of the task force.

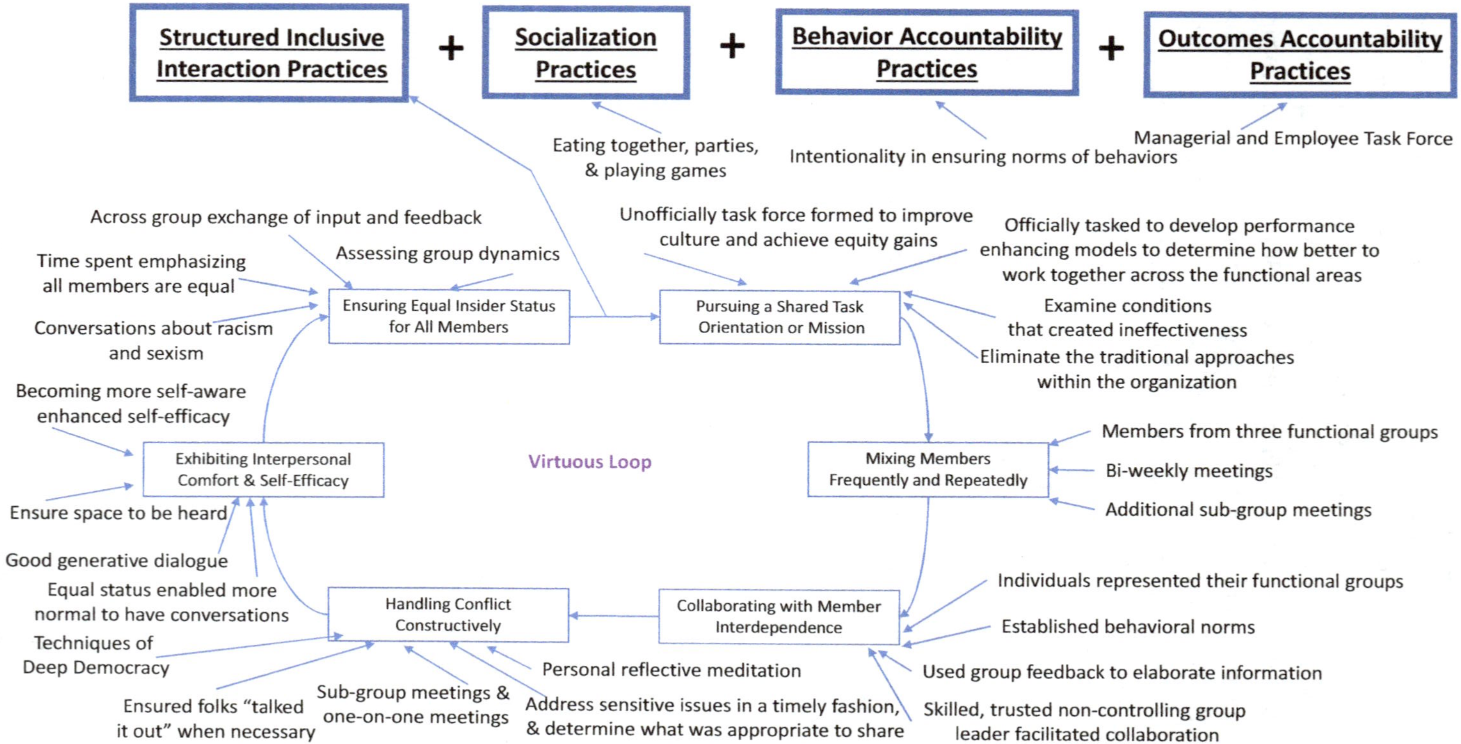

Figure 27 Cross-functional, science unit task force case

Figure 28 depicts the practices adopted by a cohort-based leadership fellowship composed of future leaders from underrepresented groups. In the cohort we examined, over a period of eighteen months, thirteen participants met twice monthly and for the occasional weekend retreat. Focusing on self-awareness, community engagement, and social/racial equity, each new group began by creating a unique set of "community agreements" to guide their interactions. This enabled the members to engage with respect and integrity as they built the trust that enabled them to speak authentically about difficult subjects such as race. Having enough time to socialize together, where the discussions were "lighter," created strong bonds within the group. As one member told us, he was able to overcome fear, learn how ignorant he was, and "deeply challenge his existing ideas and search for the truth." Adopting the structured practices for inclusive interactions, socialization, and behavior accountability drove this group to learn from each other and become more aware of each other's lived experiences and challenges.

These four mission and values-driven organizations utilized the practices presented in the framework for inclusive interactions, equity, and performance. Each organization elaborated and customized the practices to fit their unique mission, values, and structure. The complexity evident in the models is required due to the typically large number of members' activities that bear on inclusion and equity. In contrast, the Al-Anon organization (Section 7) had only one core activity – its periodic meetings – and it required many fewer structured practices for inclusive interactions. The redundancy and overlap in actions that support each of the four sets of inclusive practices, as seen in the these four cases, shows the benefit of overlapping practices in order to address the wicked problems challenging diversity, inclusion, and equity. The multitude of actions that evolved in support of the practices demonstrates how, in each case, values and mission were being consistently pursued, with the practices customized to fit each situation.

9.1.1 Persistence

Systems thinking makes clear that the effects of time are critical. The cases show the value of organizations examining and elaborating all aspects of their practices for inclusion to ensure that they evolve successfully. None of these organizations approached diversity by saying, "We did X, Y, And Z. Therefore, we are diverse and no more work needs to be done," or by being satisfied with having checked the box once they had developed a formal diversity policy statement, as we found in another case, a nonprofit arts organization. Each successful case illustrates how the members lived the inclusive values and practices and were open to reevaluating them as needed.

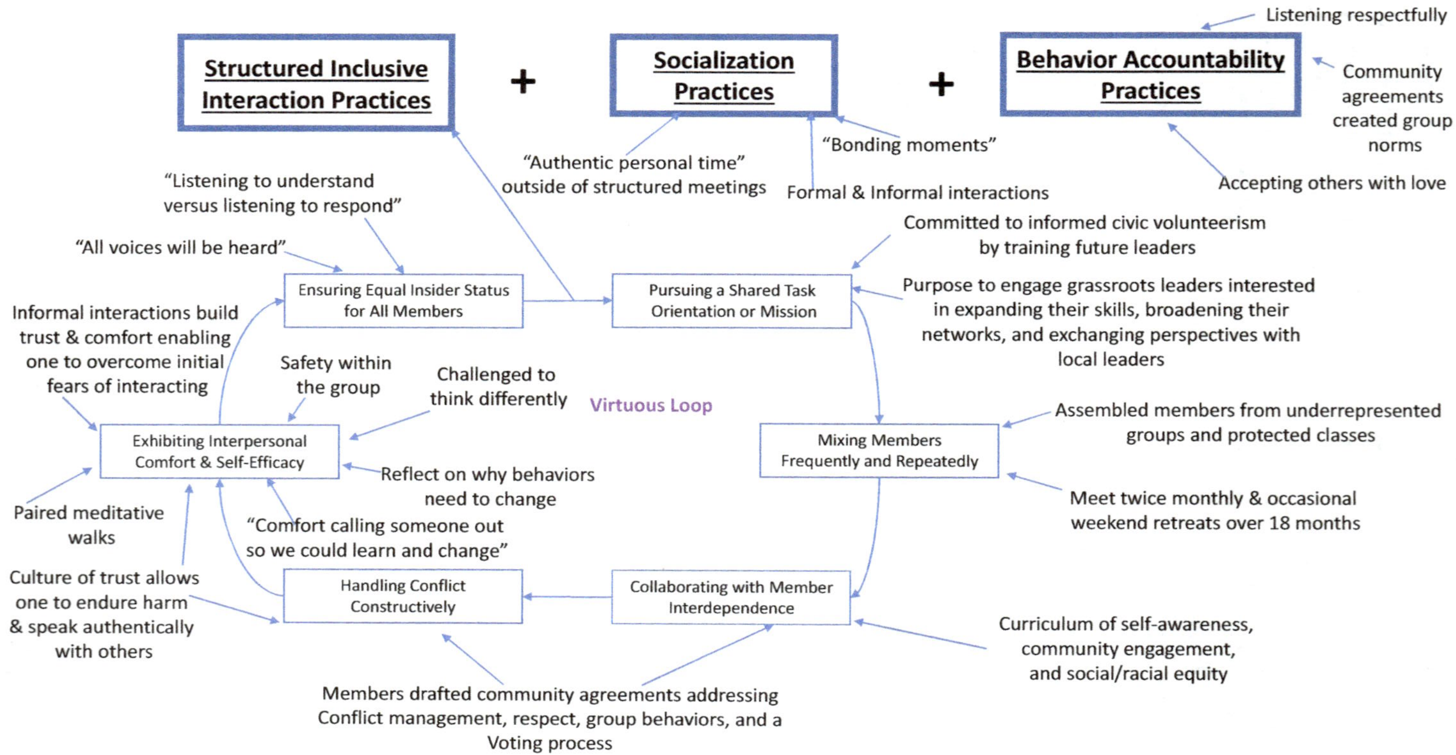

Figure 28 Leadership fellowship case

Time and persistence are important in another sense. With new cohorts entering the organization regularly, the service fraternity and medical research unit had evolved practices that enabled new members to gradually increase their trust and respect for each other. Similarly with the cross-functional change effort at the science unit, a tipping point was reached after the task force had been operating for some time. In both the leadership fellowship and science unit cases, approximately six months was noted as the time for trust development to become meaningful – that is, for adaptive learning to begin to occur.

9.1.2 Inclusion Based on Mission and Values

Comparing the four models earlier, an interesting contrast emerges between the two volunteer-driven organizations and the medical and science unit cases. The latter two organizations had outcome accountability practices while the former two did not. A possible explanation is that the volunteer-driven organizations were more able to rely on their values-driven, *fellowship-oriented* practices, including those for behavior accountability, to assure respectful and equitable behavior and outcomes among all their members.

Further, in the service fraternity, becoming diverse and inclusive was not a result of a diversity goal but, instead, of the organization's desire to meet its purpose of Service, Leadership, and Fellowship for all members. Key elements were applying its inclusive practices to everyone in the organization and, as in the science unit, promoting the practices for mission and values attainment. We concluded that these two elements diminish backlash that often follows from explicit and prescriptive diversity and inclusion efforts, as discussed in Section 4. The validity of inclusive practices being effective in sustaining diversity and inclusion is supported by the service fraternity's producing these results without intending to, by emphasizing its values of fellowship and service. Its results support the efficacy of applying inclusion and equity to all, based on mission and values.

These mission and values-driven cases achieved sustainable inclusion with increased performance outcomes that have persisted beyond the time period of our studies. Other organizations with strong missions should consider the many examples of the practices utilized here in combination with practices and activities already in use in their organizations. Plotting organizational practices on the Framework for Inclusive Interactions Equity and Performance also provides an opportunity to determine whether additional practices are needed to ensure sufficient complementarity and evolution of practices.

9.2 Nonprofit Boards of Directors

Nonprofit boards are well situated to model for their own and other organizations the efficacy of structured practices for inclusive interactions, socialization, and behavior accountability. Next we examine general boards of directors (Figure 29) and examine more closely one specific board that chose to become diverse, equitable and inclusive (Figure 30).

Nonprofit board members come together as fiduciaries because of their common interest in the organization's mission, pursuing a shared task of governing the organization to achieve its mission. Members typically meet monthly and attend organizational activities, enabling frequent and repeated interactions. Directors, as governors of their organizations, must make strategic decisions, set policy and budgets, provide legal and ethical oversight and attend to other business that advances the mission. To do this, directors must collaborate and present decisions as one.

Based on research on governing boards (Buse et al., 2016), having a diverse board improves performance, but only when inclusive behaviors and practices are present. As depicted in Figure 29, many board practices can shape members' interactions to be inclusive. Bylaws of the organization provide the rules for the board to abide by and can be used to resolve conflicts. Appropriate rules of order during meetings enable all members to participate in discussions, even when the conversations may be difficult. By ensuring that all members are respected and valued for their experiences and skills, the board can become a comfortable place to engage with differing others. Providing equal insider status for all members – as by sharing power through leadership and committee assignments – allows all members to participate meaningfully and hear a variety of perspectives. In addition, structuring opportunities for socialization at the meetings and organizational events allows members to build trust and find common interests. Behavior accountability comes from acculturating new members into the norms of the board, while outcomes accountability calls for targeted recruitment of board members from underrepresented groups, as opposed to recruiting for "fit." Fit is often a euphemism for homogeneity, favoring those who share the characteristics and perspectives of the current members.

The case of a public media nonprofit organization (Bernstein & Aspin, 2024) provides insights into successful intentional efforts to become a diverse, inclusive, and equitable board and organization. Change was initially driven by the employees, who created a task force to ensure that the organization's workforce represented its changing client demographics. The task force pressured the board to establish its own workgroup to drive strategic planning around diversity, inclusion, and equity. As depicted in Figure 30, the board then evolved

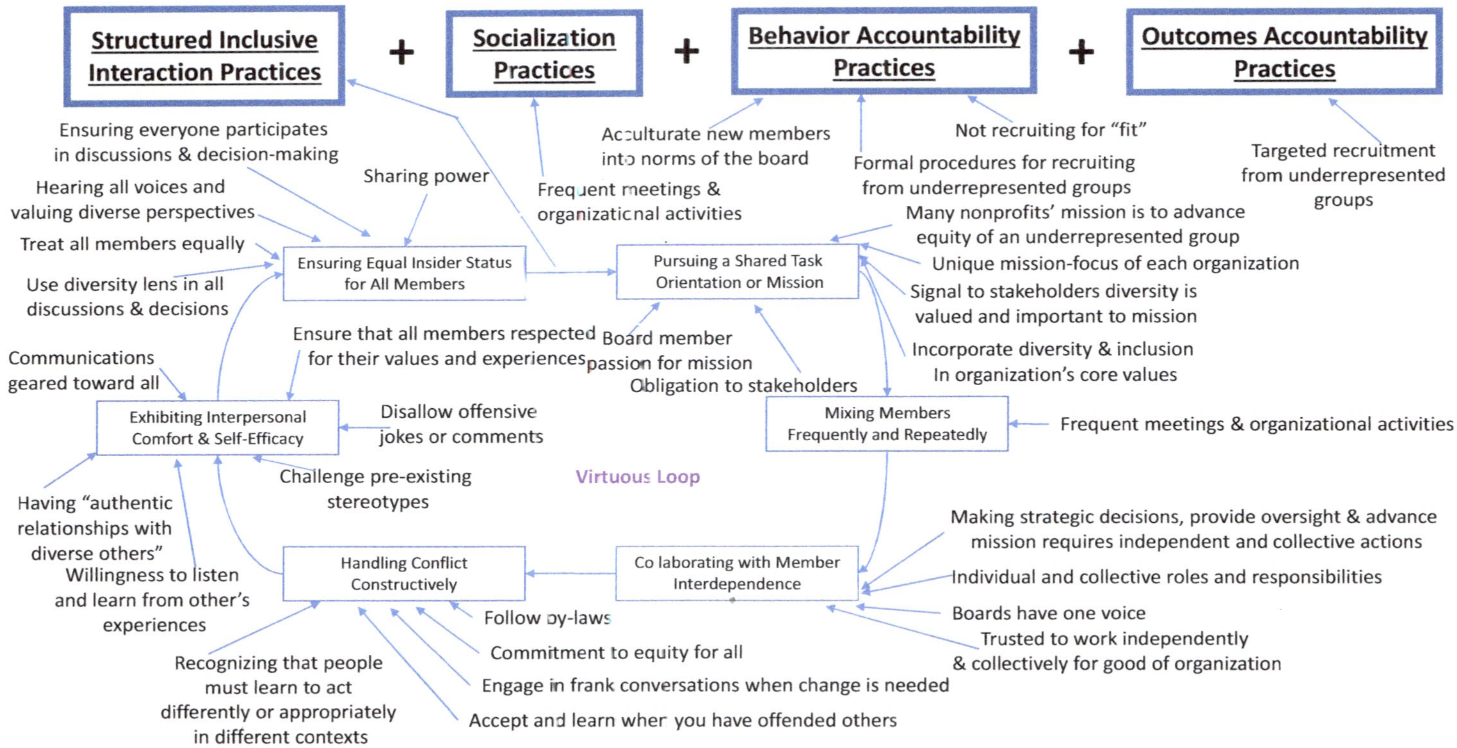

Figure 29 Boards of directors of nonprofit organizations case

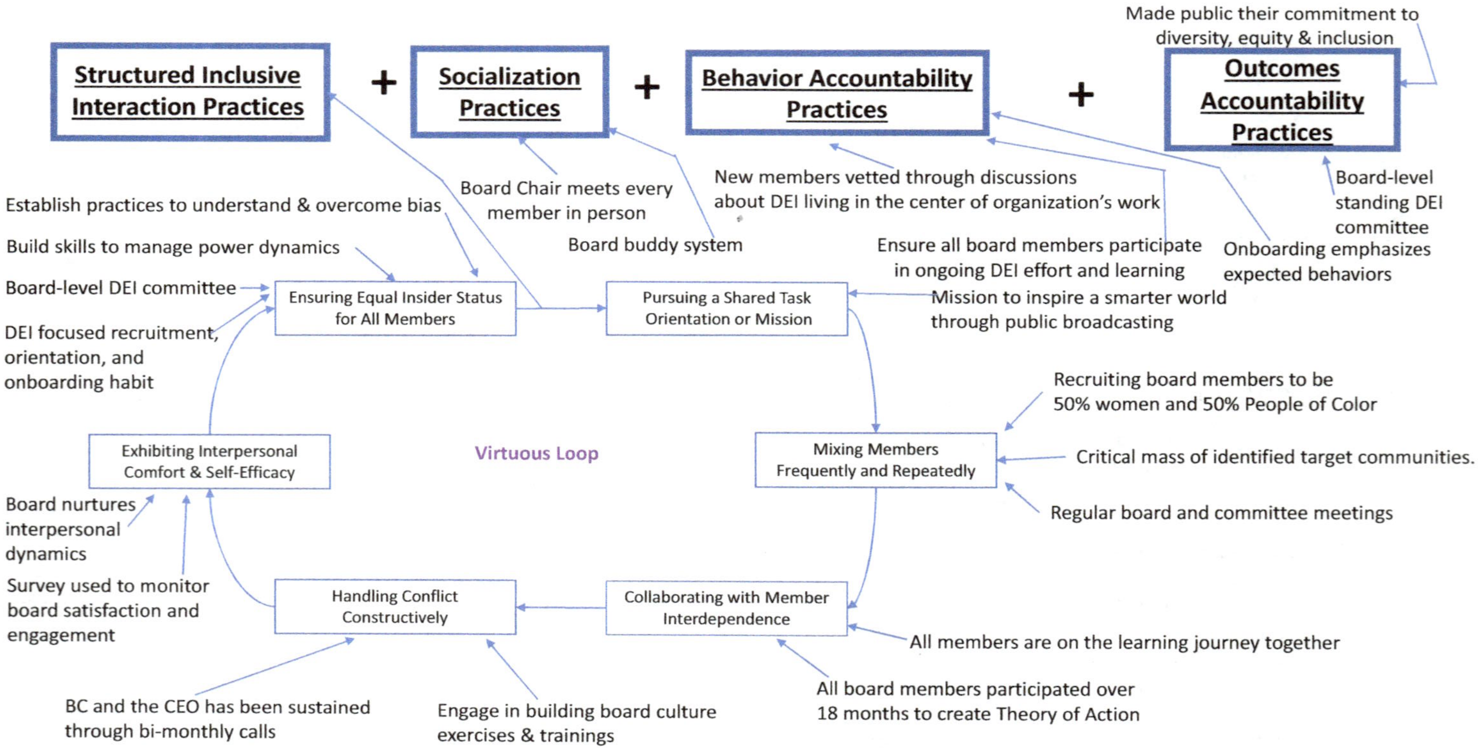

Figure 30 Public media board of directors case

multiple practices, striving for an environment where everyone is valued, able to share their experiences, and equipped to talk about diversity, equity and inclusion. Consistent with the client case for diversity, they recognized this work as a business imperative driven by the shifting needs and aspirations of the entire community they served, including a younger and more diverse population. After extensive examination of other diverse and inclusive boards and working with a consultant, the board, over eighteen months, produced an accountability-driven strategic framework that brought an equity lens to all aspects of governance. The goal was to bring new recruits to the board that had no prior board experience, to leverage their experiential diversity and distinct ideas. Beyond "walking the talk," board members felt the need to "live" these changes by "going beyond checking boxes" to using diversity, equity and inclusion as a lens through which decisions are made, similar to applying a legal or budgetary lens. The formation of a standing diversity, equity and inclusion committee at the board level provided ongoing accountability and ensured the desired impact: a diverse, multigenerational, and engaged board.

The public media board, with its broad emphasis on diversity, equity and inclusion, may be viewed as a plan of action for boards desiring to be more inclusive. The commitment begins with recruiting for diversity and not "fit," ensuring that new directors are made aware of expected respectful behaviors within the group, and having policies that disallow exclusive behaviors and speech. Mentors may be needed if the new directors have never served on a board. Mixing of the members at the meetings, on committees, and in social situations fosters comfort among the members, contributing to everyone having equal status. While boards serve differing missions, they are all performance driven and, as noted in Section 1, the results argument for diversity applies to them all. Leveraging a diversity of thought, lived experiences and skills on the board is crucial for success.

In contrast to the board of director cases presented here, board members and consultants have told us of boards that have not had success with diversifying. Two common situations repeatedly arose. In the first, the "check the box" approach, the boards would create a "diversity" plan and then not use it to change their actions or behaviors. They were able to say that they had a diversity plan, but nothing changed with respect to governing the organization. In the second situation, the boards simply did not even start to create a diversity plan, stating that they were too busy working on budgeting, bylaw revisions, strategic planning, and so on. This perspective failed to consider the value of incorporating diversity into all actions of the board – having a lens through which decision-making and discussions would always consider diversity, equity and inclusion, in the same manner as having a financial or legal lens.

9.3 A Case of Top-Down-Driven Change

Figure 31, provides an example of organization-wide diversity, equity and inclusion efforts driven by a governmental unit's leader. A military base with thousands of civilian and military employees was assigned their first female Commanding Officer who implemented a new graphically depicted strategic plan that emphasized organizational values. The base had experienced conflict primarily around gender and generational issues. For example, men often had difficulties with women in traditionally "male" jobs such as welding and crane operation. The elder employees viewed Gen Z and millennials as lazier. The strategic plan, designed to reduce the conflict and prejudices, was created with and depicted by the organization's vision, mission, results, and strategies surrounded by the guiding organizational values of integrity, teamwork, ingenuity, excellence, and service. Input from all levels of the workforce went into the plan. Supervisors were introduced to the new plan and trained on how to articulate and model the framework. The Commanding Officer's behavior and her "shake things up" attitude put everyone on notice that they were going to "stop using old ineffective methods" in order to create an inclusive culture that is "a safe environment for all." In contrast to the science unit case, the top leadership, with buy-in from the workforce, set the tone for, and influenced, acceptable behaviors, changing the culture of the military base.

As is clear from the research findings modeled in Sections 4 and 5, a severe challenge to a top-down initiative for diversity, inclusion, and equity is the likelihood of resistance and backlash from employees and middle-level managers. That challenge clearly exists for the military base. However, several actions offer promise that inclusive and equitable practices will be sustained. These include: the modeling of behaviors by the Commanding Officer; steps taken to ensure behavioral and outcomes accountability, such as creating a hotline for reporting issues; training of the middle-level managers in the importance of using the plan to improve performance; and efforts made to get input from all functional areas in creating the plan. It is possible that this facility, with its comparatively high gender and generational differences and low racial diversity, may have had greater backlash and less successful outcomes with different employee demographics. As at the science unit, a further step that could have been taken to mitigate backlash is the establishing of a cross-level, cross-functional task force focused on diagnosing performance-related interaction problems and promoting inclusion for all.

9.4 Elaborating and Customizing Practices for Inclusion

Taken together the cases illustrate the various ways in which these public and nonprofit organizations have implemented the structured practices for inclusive

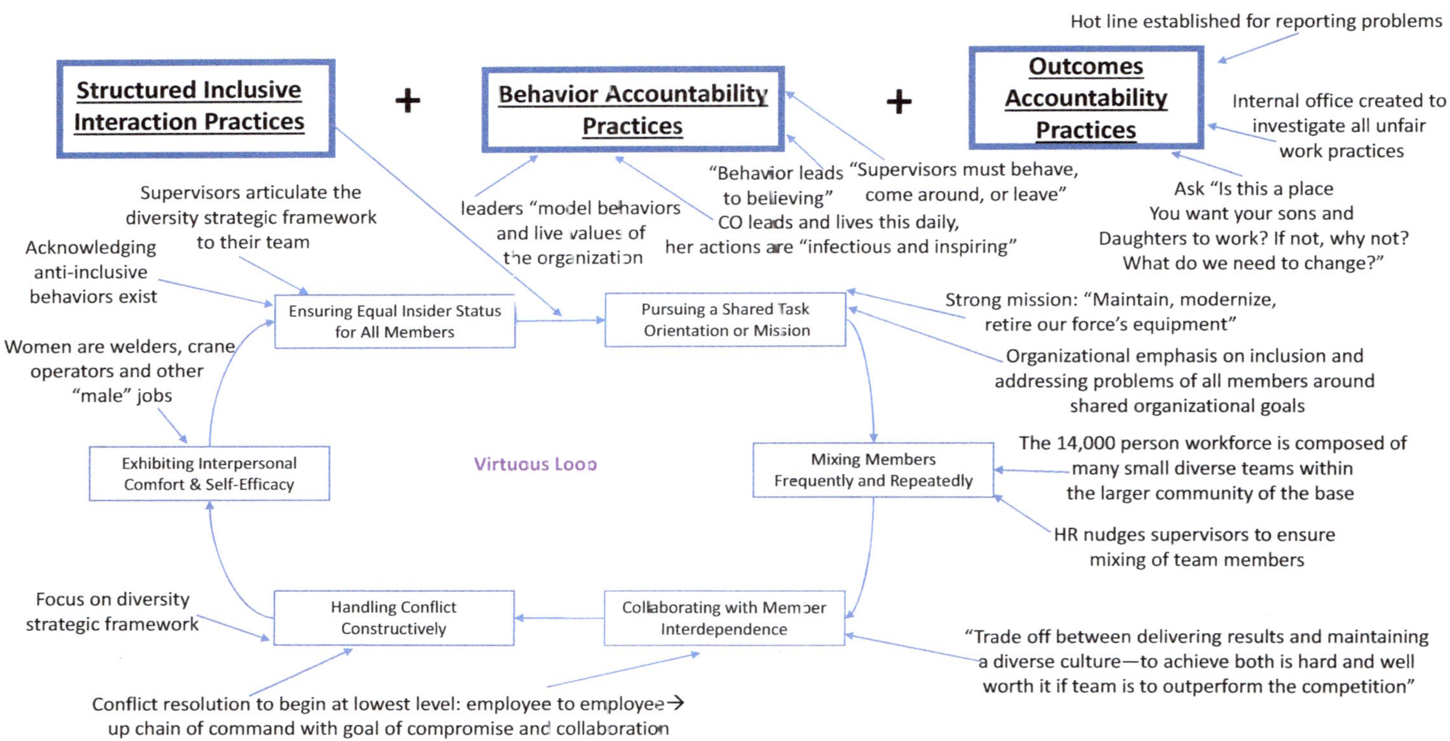

Figure 31 Military base case

interactions, socialization, behavior accountability, and outcomes accountability depicted in the framework for inclusive interactions, equity, and performance. By modeling the system dynamics of these cases, we are able to visualize the multitude of actions used to support each practice. The feedback loops and delays make it easy to identify the need for the practices and actions to persist, and for them to be elaborated and evolved to meet the needs of the specific organization and its members. The cases demonstrate that there exist many mutually reinforcing practices, in varying forms available for use in different organizations.

Because diversity (representation) alone is insufficient for improving performance and equity, the practices for inclusive interactions are understood as the primary and frequently neglected leverage point for change. These interaction practices work in combination with the socialization and behavior and outcomes accountability practices to achieve sustainable inclusion. We anticipate that these cases provide a vast array of practices that may be adapted and applied to foster inclusion across the public and nonprofit sectors.

Creating an inclusive workgroup, board or organization takes persistence with inclusive practices and values. For example, in the service fraternity achieving inclusion with diversity was not intended. However, despite the inclusive practices and values being designed for a homogeneous group, because they were applied persistently and for all members, they worked for a diverse group as well.

9.5 Initiating Change

A mission-oriented pursuit of inclusion and equity was the norm in the earlier cases, but note that its initiative can come from the top, middle, or bottom of the organizational hierarchy, and its motivation can be any one or more of the arguments for diversity with inclusion and equity (Section 1). The public media case is especially notable because the drive to become a diverse, inclusive and equitable board and organization was employee driven/bottom-up and argued as necessary to better serve its market. We have observed greater success with organizations that have employee or staff input in diversity plans or initiatives. In the military base case, we see a top-down diversity plan argued as necessary to counter interaction conflict, with member input and "buy-in" that proved successful, while in the science unit the drive for change was middle-out, driven by leaders of the functional groups and staff facilitators concerned with disrespectful interactions that impeded unit performance. Performance was the "official" rationale needed to gain the go-ahead for the change project from the science organization's leaders.

In these cases, we saw a reduction in backlash against the diversity change efforts, highlighting the value of employee groups initiating change and pushing higher level leaders to act. We hypothesize that the mission and values-focus of nonprofit and public sector organizations might create more employee and staff support for meaningful inclusion and equity. In the case of the public media board, the standing diversity committee should keep the board accountable, resulting in more inclusion and less discrimination within the board itself. The presence of this committee should make it more likely that the board will persist in supporting inclusion throughout the organization.

With the large body of research that has established how prescriptive policies for diversity trigger and sustain backlash that undermines their effectiveness (Sections 4 and 5), individuals and organizations should be mindful about the ways in which they initiate and promote changes for diversity and inclusion. Several overlapping threads running through the earlier cases provide guidance on mitigating backlash:

- Emphasizing mission attainment and related organizational values encourages members to focus on respectfully leveraging each other's differing talents and perspectives.
- Succeeding with a diverse set of stakeholders benefits from a mirrored diversity in the members that work in and govern the organization, providing a mission-attainment reason for pursuing diversity with inclusion and equity.
- Tensions and conflicts related to differing perspectives are to be expected from diversity, and valued, but they call for practices of collaboration, conflict-handling, and behavior accountability that lead to constructive outcomes and sustain trusting, respectful relationships. Because these practices are central to superior mission attainment, they apply to all interactions among members, not only to diversity interactions.

10 Policymaking, Research, and Practice: Systems Thinking Insights for Diversity Success

Applying concepts and tools from systems thinking and intergroup contact theory, in this monograph we have attempted to analyze diversity's challenges and prospects. Drawing on empirical research from many fields revealing problems and opportunities, an overall conclusion is clear: The realities of lack of progress with diversity and equity over many decades require researchers and leaders to inquire into and apply a wider range of diversity policies and practices in order to overcome policy resistance. Achieving inclusion, equity, and performance from diversity calls for experimentation that is not limited to

Table 9 Section 10 figures

Figure Number	Description
32	Actions and processes at the societal level, including political and legal, support anti-inclusive social practices that organizational leaders must overcome to achieve inclusion. Within organizations, backlash to prescriptive diversity, equity and inclusion policies further inhibits inclusive interactions, rendering diversity interactions infrequent and superficial.
33	Guidance from systems thinking modeling for leaders and managers: The value of persistent organizational commitment in combining, elaborating, and evolving practices that result in sustainable inclusion, equity, and superior mission performance.

informative studies by social psychological researchers but also pursued by leaders in organizational practice. Organizational scholars can contribute to more effective practice through broadened field research inquiring into combinations of practices that fit differing organizational and community settings. Case studies of successful organizations can suggest additional forms of practices and change efforts that reduce prejudices and boost equity and mission attainment. The figures presented in this section are described in Table 9.

Experimentation by organizations need not wait for further research. Based on existing bodies of knowledge from multiple academic disciplines and fields and the successful nonprofit and public sector cases, promising alternatives to current policies are available for application in a broad range of organizations. Based on this knowledge, institutional and organizational leaders can encourage experimentation at the work unit level, enabling adaptations that fit the mission, local community and work context of the organizational unit and its members.

An important lesson emerges from applying systems thinking to organizations' pursuit of diversity policies: Due to unanticipated dynamics typical of social systems, leaders' persistence is required to evolve and sustain effective diversity policies, just as it is for all other serious concerns, such as budget management and service delivery. Extending the past work on motivations for pursuing diversity (Section 1), research can inquire into the nature and sources of effective persistence by leaders, with leaders being guided by a focus on their system's dynamics. Ongoing diagnosing and revising are necessary to overcome unintended follow-on effects. Successfully shaping organizational members' social practices for inclusion and equity rests on a continuing series of diagnoses, decisions and actions by policymakers and managers, striving to align work unit conditions and values in ways that produce mission attainment from diverse talents and perspectives. Leaders' diagnoses benefit by being aware of the competing dynamics over time of inclusive and anti-inclusive practices. Because anti-inclusive practices are carried into the organization from the broader society, limited attainment of inclusion, equity, and performance from diversity is the default that leaders and researchers can expect without counter-vailing organizational efforts. The modeling of research findings and cases in the sections earlier communicates a variety of understandings for policymakers concerned with the basic questions presented at the beginning of this monograph: Why has progress stalled and what policy alternatives promise better success?

One response, given the many problematic social forces that undermine contemporary efforts, is that more attention should be given to combinations of practices that, over time, counteract those forces. For example, on their own, fair employment practices such as job tests for promotions lead to member interpretations that undermine diversity success. However, when properly timed and in combination with elaborated sets of inclusive practices that reduce prejudices, fair employment practices have the potential to contribute, instead, to equity, sustained inclusion, and unit performance.

With the notable exception of studies by Kalev, Dobbin, and colleagues (Dobbin et al., 2015; Kalev, 2009: Kalev et al., 2006) and by Castilla (2015), too little research has examined the effects of diversity policies over time. From these few studies, and from case analyses, we see that many elements of intentional diversity initiatives are ineffective or counter-effective yet continue to be used. Meanwhile, in contrast, we see some organizations succeeding with diversity, inclusion, and equity through practices they have evolved over time to achieve mission and values rather than to achieve diversity goals. As in Castilla's study of a managerial task force and the science unit and public media board cases earlier, research is needed on mission-driven change processes in contemporary organizations that produce successful evolution of diversity with equity and inclusion.

10.1 Policy Challenges Revealed by Research and System Dynamics

The dynamic models presented earlier point to a wide range of phenomena that affect the evolution and success or failure of diversity initiatives. Combining effects from the models generates understandings for the now-historical lack of progress on diversity and aids leaders and researchers in diagnosing current problems. However, representing and communicating the combined effects in two-dimensional models is difficult, due to the large number of elements and their many connections. As one example of combining effects, in the following paragraphs we synthesize in words (rather than a highly complex model) a number of relationships that bear on the dynamic reproduction of stereotyping and stigmatizing, and on the inequities and disparities that they persistently produce. As we modeled in a simplified fashion in Figure 13, systems thinking involves an interplay over time among dominant group members' attitudes and actions and those of underrepresented group members.

Negative stereotypes of underrepresented group members' competence and associated stigmatizing by dominant group individuals leads the latter group to make lower assessments of underrepresented group members' performance and their potential for higher-level positions. In turn, those lower assessments result in fewer opportunities being offered to underrepresented groups for personal development and promotions. Those fewer opportunities for advancement keep underrepresented groups crowded into lower status occupations, which maintains stereotypes of underrepresented groups as less capable, completing one vicious feedback loop. The crowding into lower status positions also decreases the chances for underrepresented group members to be in higher level positions where they can provide support to underrepresented groups at lower levels, thereby diminishing a potential buffer (Meadows, 2008) and its associated virtuous feedback loop. Another vicious loop involves lower assessments of performance leading to underrepresented groups receiving lower pay. Consistent with equity theory (Mowday, 1991), the lower economic rewards, when perceived by underrepresented groups as inequitable, reduce their incentives to perform at a high level, since higher performance is not rewarded by the organization. Some underrepresented group members then lower their performance efforts to match the level of rewards they receive. Others leave the organization, some to pursue entrepreneurship, again reducing support for those underrepresented group members remaining in the organization. Not only do these phenomena reinforce stereotypes of low competence, they also maintain erroneous beliefs in meritocracy. Those beliefs lead dominant group members to see diversity initiatives as inequitable and to mask consciousness of their implicit bias. Consequently, they attribute the lower occupational status of underrepresented groups to lower competence, completing this additional vicious loop.

For members of underrepresented groups, the most insidious phenomenon is the internalizing of lower competence (Leslie et al., 2014). Being stereotyped and stigmatized tends to lower self-assessments of one's performance, leading some to accept the lower rewards they receive as appropriate and to fail to seek career development and advancement opportunities, keeping them in lower-status, low reward positions that maintain negative stereotypes. These dynamics further sustain beliefs in meritocracy, even among some underrepresented group members.

As noted in Section 3, one explanation offered for employment inequalities is that they are due to personal choices, such as women choosing to attend to family over career. The system dynamics described in Sections 4 and 5 indicate how stereotyping and bias in personnel decisions serve to reproduce that explanation. When lower employment rewards are perceived by underrepresented group members as due to discrimination, they have less economic incentive to make occupational and career investments whose payoffs depend on employers' biased decisions. Alternatively, if they perceive their lower rewards to be a meritocratic result of lower capabilities, they are similarly less likely to invest in career development. Consequently, observed group differences in qualifications can be interpreted by onlookers as personal choices that explain inequalities, but in reality, the group disparities have as an important underlying cause the operation of bias and inequitable rewards. In this way and others, negative stereotyping is not only imported into the organization from the broader society, it is also exported from the organization to the society. The societal and organizational dynamics are mutually reinforcing.

These discussions capture only some of the phenomena modeled earlier that reproduce stereotyping, associated inequities, and unfounded beliefs in meritocracy. Knowledge of the various phenomena producing unintended effects can inform policymakers and researchers operating in a particular organizational context, enabling them to be aware of the nuances of powerful system dynamics as they attempt to diagnose shortfalls in diversity efforts (Figure 2). Drawing on the variety of forms of practices found in Section 9's cases, they can then consider how best to examine, initiate, and evolve in their context the four sets of inclusive practices specified in our overall framework (Figures 16, 17, and 19 through 21). To interrupt the reproduction of stereotyping and inequities in rewards and advancement, they can devote particular attention to inclusive interactions at the work unit level. The framework recognizes, through a feedback loop, the need to pay constant attention to supporting inclusive practices and nurturing a collaborative, mission-attainment culture in the work environment. Otherwise, adaptive learning will be undermined by the self-reinforcing feedback loops of anti-inclusive practices that are constantly supported by external societal structures and processes.

10.2 A Primary Leverage Point: Emphasizing Work Unit Performance via Inclusive Interaction Practices

Meadows (2008) notes that sometimes we have to give up on current policies, finding instead a leverage point that is promising so that we do not give up on what we want to accomplish collectively. The preceding analyses lead to a main leverage point and a path forward for achieving diversity that differs substantially from current diversity efforts – namely, the shared goal of mission attainment and its payoffs for individual members.

Regarding "giving up," the core implication of research and modeling concerning the unintended effects of common diversity policies is that policy revision is needed that somehow avoids, greatly minimizes, or counters the self-fulfilling, policy-resistant interpretations that explicit diversity policies trigger among many workforce members. Those interpretations sustain self-segregating, stereotyping, stigmatizing, and making decisions based on implicit bias. As discussed earlier, bodies of research tell us that attempts within organizations to change negative attitudes directly, as through mandatory diversity training, have proven ineffective or counter-effective, a finding that is consistent with the ubiquitous operation of implicit, largely subconscious bias. Consequently, the challenge is to achieve the goals of diversity, equity, and inclusion through less direct methods, adopting policies that concentrate on effective means rather than on direct attacks against undesired ends.

Consistent with a history of system dynamics analyses leading to solutions rooted in operational structures and processes, system dynamics modeling of research findings points to the neglected leverage point of structuring work practices that lead to strong unit performance through frequent, productive member interactions. Here, we highlight a key aspect of this effective structuring – its *explicit emphasis on unit performance and mission attainment rather than on diversity goals*. As found in several of the cases reviewed earlier, sustaining productive diversity interactions results from structuring productive, respectful interactions among all members. In a Silicon Valley tech firm (a for-profit organization), we found that leaders promoted behavior accountability practices as rooted in performance because they had learned about the destructive effects of conflictual interactions within their workforce. The emphasis on performance-favoring practices that involve all unit members – such as personalized socialization that identifies each member's work-relevant skills and knowledge (Cable et al., 2013) – has positive impacts on diversity interactions without singling out those interactions and triggering undermining interpretations, as do direct, prescriptive diversity efforts.

In recent decades interpretations that undermine inclusion and equity have been reinforced by political actions and legal constraints around explicit diversity initiatives. In many countries the issue has centered on immigration. In some states in the United States, actions associated with the term "DEI" (Diversity, Equity, and Inclusion), such as discussions of social justice in public educational institutions, have been prohibited by laws. Various examples of such political actions are represented in Figure 32 as contributing to the dynamic processes by

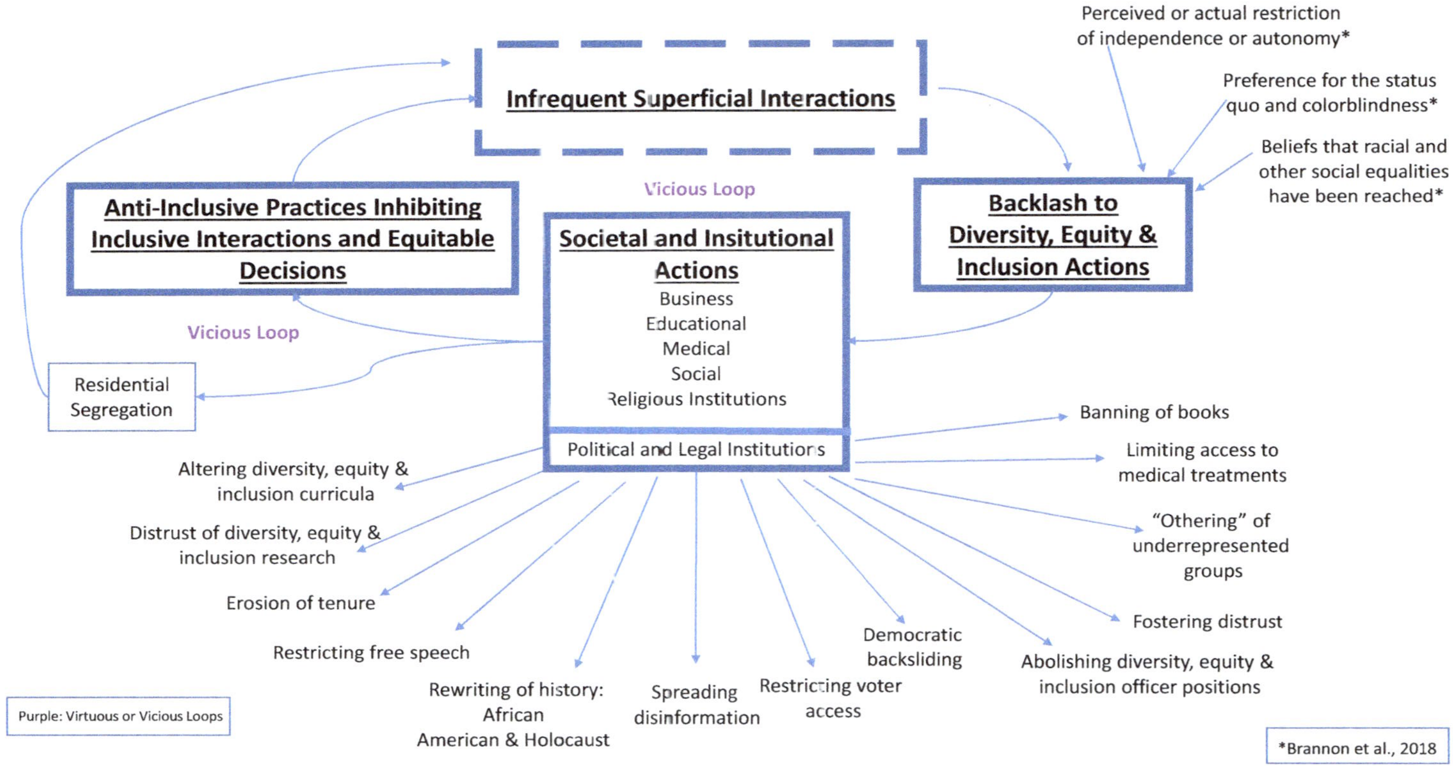

Figure 32 Impacts of societal actions and processes

which anti-inclusive practices and superficial diversity interactions are sustained within organizations and societies. These societal processes carry risks for organizational members who develop close intergroup friendships at work, since research finds that they may be criticized for those friendships by their own families and within-group friends (Marinucci et al., 2021).

The inclusion-undermining interpretations that follow from explicit diversity policies threaten the effectiveness of some formal mentoring, championing, and support group practices for underrepresented groups. Support groups within organizations have been found to benefit the advancement of women but to harm that of Black men (Kalev et al., 2006). To avoid these types of backlash effects, one solution is for support groups to operate outside of the work organization, through informal networks or externally based organizations such as the Divine Nine sororities and fraternities for Black students and adults (Greyerbiehl & Mitchell, 2014; Hernandez, 2008). Creating more such supporting organizations is an opportunity for the nonprofit sector. And, networking and championing within the organization can be decoupled from explicit diversity efforts through the results-motivated structuring of performance-oriented inclusive practices, such as collaboration and cross-job training (Kalev, 2009). These practices create new networks of informal personal relationships across organizational levels, improving the advancement of underrepresented group members while enhancing organizational coordination and performance.

The leverage point of mission-focused inclusion for performance carries with it an emphasis on win-win outcomes for organizational members. One explanation offered for backlash interpretations common at the societal and organizational levels is that diversity and inclusion efforts are viewed from a zero-sum perspective (Brannon et al., 2018) – one group perceives that their situation must worsen for another group's situation to improve. Promoting inclusive practices for work unit performance and organizational mission attainment, and as applying to all members, can shift the perspective toward win-win benefits, with superior mission attainment and personal growth being satisfying and of value to many members of public and nonprofit organizations. As in the medical research unit case (Section 9), leaders can link inclusive practices to sets of rewards that are of personal benefit to each sub-unit of workers.

Support for the work structuring, mission attainment-based approach to inclusion comes not only from case studies but also from the previously cited longitudinal quantitative analyses of major U.S. companies finding that cross-job training and self-directed work teams lead to improved advancement of underrepresented groups (Kalev, 2009). An informative parallel is agile teams in software development (Dyba & Dingsoyr, 2008), adopted by information technology groups to provide superior performance. These teams utilize many structured interaction processes – such as the collaborative, mixing process of pair programming where two members develop code together (Hummel et al., 2015) – that match the six inclusive practices specified in our framework.

Case studies of nonprofit and public organizations demonstrate that achieving inclusion and equity for members of underrepresented groups is highly feasible when inclusive practices are promoted and adopted on the basis of improved unit performance and organizational values. The bottom-line requirement is that the practices apply to and provide inclusion and benefits for all members, including those from underrepresented groups. For diversity officers and other organizational leaders, advocating these all-member practices as an effective means of mission attainment offers an alternative leverage point to problematic diversity-explicit policies. As we found with a number of our cases, valuing mission attainment represents a shared goal and an overarching paradigm that can be leveraged for diversity with inclusion and equity. With goals and paradigms being identified by Meadows (2008) as two of the three most powerful leverage points, many nonprofit and public sector organizations have the comparative advantage over for-profit organizations of members sharing in the paradigm of mission attainment, given their beliefs that the collective efforts will contribute to society.

10.3 Ongoing Policy Persistence and Revision

A major accountability failure is current diversity policymaking ignoring the research-based evidence that many contemporary diversity policies are ineffective, and have been for decades, with some policies hurting, rather than helping, the employment outcomes for underrepresented groups. What accounts for organizations persisting with diversity policies that produce limited and eroding success?

As noted earlier, one answer heard from interviewees in our cases is that leaders simply "check the box" of pursuing commonly accepted diversity policies, based on legal compliance and public relations concerns. Another answer is that leaders may perceive more effective, interaction-increasing practices as being difficult to establish and not worth the effort, yet our cases demonstrate not only their feasibility but also their performance advantages in nonprofit and public organizations. The fact that some organizations – in our cases, the coed service fraternity and the leadership fellowship – routinely succeed in creating inclusion and equity with new cohorts suggests that effective change is realistic. So, too, the successful change efforts at the science unit and military base. Another possible explanation for diversity policy rigidity is that leaders may fear that policies centered on increasing intergroup interactions will produce negative reactions, but as found in Schafer et al.'s (2021) review, studies indicate that negative reactions to actual contact are relatively infrequent and leaders should err on the side of creating more rather than less contact. Further, our cases indicate that combinations of the framework's inclusive practices make negative reactions even less likely.

As discussed in Section 2, system dynamics suggests additional answers to the issue of policy rigidity. Individuals tend to rely on simplistic causal models that postulate a single effect of an action (Sterman, 2002), failing to anticipate or react to unintended follow-on effects. In approaching any complex system, individuals make decisions based on the information they have at the time, lacking perfect or complete information (Simon, 1996), often leading to poor decisions (Meadows, 2008). This results in living with faultily-made policy and behavior choices, and to individuals self-justifying their past choices (Staw, 1976), changing behavior only when forced to do so. In interviews we conducted in a variety of settings, across the sectors, interviewees noted, gratefully, that being in diverse workgroups "forced" them to interact with diverse others. In hindsight they were grateful to have experienced positive, behavior-altering, inclusive interactions over extended periods of time. In contrast, people typically tend to make decisions based on comfort and recent experiences "rather than long-term behavior," inhibiting behavioral changes that would occur if more complete, timelier, and better information were sought and utilized (Meadows, 2008, pp. 107–108).

The Framework (Figure 1) highlights the significance of designing effective practices for inclusion and equity by identifying and attending to system dynamics, including information gained from feedback loops. However, when designing at any one point in time, "The information delivered by a feedback loop can only affect future behavior; it can't deliver a signal fast enough to correct behavior that drove the current feedback" (Meadows, 2008, p. 39). This means there will always be delays in responding. Diagnosing, designing, and implementing is a continuing process, with each learned redesign of practices likely to lead to both the desired intended effects and unwanted policy resistance, as in the multiple unanticipated, unintended effects discussed in Sections 4 and 5. Consequently, as in many areas of managerial concern, persistent commitment to diagnosing and redesigning is required to gradually produce and sustain desired results.

Cases analyzed in Section 9 revealed that approximately six months of repeated interactions are needed for stereotypes to be challenged and attitudes to change. This time delay is necessary for a complex system's behavior to begin to be altered. Leaders can keep in mind that "changing the length of a delay may utterly change the behavior" of a system (Meadows, 2008, p. 104). Since member discomfort, resistance and awkwardness can be expected with any changed workgroup practice, it is valuable for leaders, as in the medical research unit case, to periodically convey commitment and provide short-term, positive feedback to workgroup members on the developing, mission-relevant success of the new practices (Repenning & Sterman, 2002), sustaining commitment to further improve inclusive, productive practices (Figure 33).

Delays in effects are inherent to the dynamics of complex systems. They carry important implications for the timing of policy actions. The concept of delays provides a way for policy to cope with a paradox: Outcomes accountability practices appear necessary to identify and deal with bias in final personnel decisions on pay, development, and promotions (Castilla, 2015), yet monitoring outcomes to check on the attaining of equity represents an explicit focus on diversity, producing the unintended dynamics that sustain stereotypes and implicit bias (Sections 4 and 5). We propose one way to address the paradox: initially, take advantage of the other three sets of inclusive practices, as depicted in Figure 33, and delay practices for outcomes accountability until the first three practices produce prejudice reduction. As emphasized earlier, the three practices – those for inclusive interactions, socialization, and behavior accountability – can be promoted on performance goals rather than diversity goals and applied to interactions of all members. Following Figure 2, the three practices can be refined until meaningful reductions in prejudices are being achieved. At that point, with managers' personnel decisions becoming less biased, leaders can initiate a managerial task force to monitor outcomes accountability.

More broadly, task forces are a valuable mechanism for dealing with delays in effects, as evidenced by the important role they played in producing sustained change in several of our cases. Their efficacy matches the finding from a review of studies that challenges such as intergroup contact anxiety can be mitigated by within-group support for both ingroup and outgroup members (Kauff et al., 2021). As the members of diverse task forces develop trust in each other over time, they can provide support for others in their groups to engage in more frequent intergroup contact, as seen in our science unit case.

10.4 Qualifications

While our analyses are evidence-based, they are subject to critique. One critique is that the modeling reflects the general effects found in studies, but these general effects should not be seen as applying to all individuals and contexts. For example, some studies have found that individual and geographical

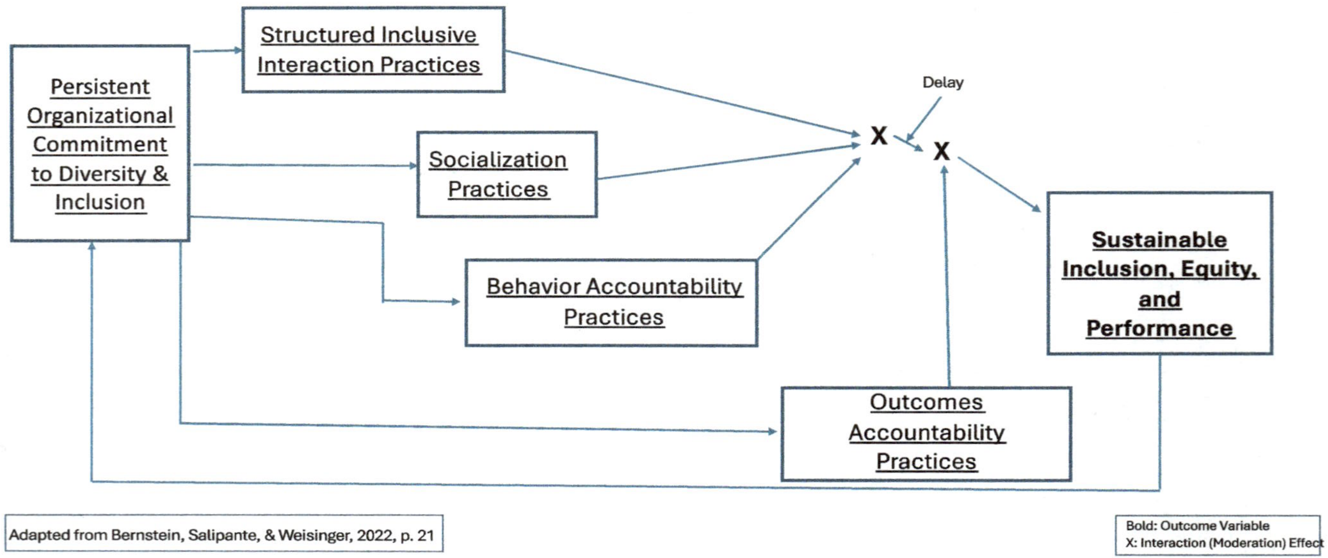

Figure 33 Practices for inclusive interactions, equity, and performance

differences can affect the degree of prejudice reduction resulting from intergroup contact, with the prejudice-reducing effects of contact being lower for individuals with more negative views of outgroups (Paluck et al., 2019). Surprisingly, for such individuals the transfer to other groups and individuals of the positive effects of contact has been found to be greater (Boin et al., 2021).

Another example of the limitations of general effects concerns the research finding, noted earlier, that the general effect of being stereotyped and stigmatized is a lowering of self-assessed performance. However, as exemplified by mid-career executives in our doctoral educational programs, individuals can retain their self-efficacy despite having experienced such treatment in the workplace. Challenging beliefs that our organizations are fair and meritocratic, they attribute the treatment to others' bias and resolve to overcome it by seeking further education, knowledge, and credentials. Support groups within and outside the organization, such as Black sororities, reinforce these attributions.

Another critique is that particular of our cases reflect organizational contexts that are distinctive and that favor the effects of inclusive practices, such as voluntary organizations (e.g., the coed service fraternity) where members may have less of a stake than were the organization their employer. The variety of nonprofit and public organizations in which we find success with inclusive practices softens this critique. Still, each type of organization will have its challenges in succeeding with inclusive practices and will benefit from policy persistence to find inclusive practices that work in its context.

As discussed earlier, a related critique is that inclusive practices will often not be effective. One possibility is that the societal reinforcement of anti-inclusive practices will have such strong impact on both dominant group and underrepresented group members that it will counter-act the prejudice reduction effects of inclusive practices inside the organization. Indeed, we have modeled behavior inside the organization as a competition between anti-inclusive practices prevalent in society with inclusive practices structured by the organization. Since studies of intergroup contact find that the prejudice-reducing effects of contact generalize in several ways, there is every chance that inclusive practices experienced in an organization will change individuals' behaviors and attitudes there and elsewhere, but societal forces should not be underestimated.

Another challenge to effectiveness is that the delays noted in our models will result in members of underrepresented groups departing the organization or, for those who remain, paying a price until newly initiated inclusive practices succeed. Further research is needed to assess the length of delays and the nature of change processes that retain individuals by offering sufficient hope of improvement in inclusion and equity, as was found in the science unit case. Regarding change processes, research should further investigate the role of task forces and consultants, since internal staff consultants played a key role in that case and an external consultant similarly facilitated change in the Public Media Board case.

With challenges to the efficacy of inclusive practices being real and ongoing, we call for a combination of new organizational practice and new research. Future practice and research can center on new workplace approaches to inclusion and equity, approaches informed by the existing research-based evidence and real-life cases such as those modeled earlier.

10.5 Future Organizational Practice and Research

From our experiences applying systems thinking modeling to inclusion, equity, and mission attainment, we draw several conclusions regarding the persistent sources of problems and leverage points available for use and inquiry:

(1) A large body of research from many fields of study demonstrates the dynamic complexities of diversity phenomena, explaining policy resistance and the reproduction of problems over many decades.
(2) Models of systems dynamics, based on research evidence and depicting causal loops, can match the complexity of diversity systems' wicked problems. Systems thinking modeling encourages the specification of problematic dynamics typically lacking in diversity research, dynamics that favor a leverage point of pursuing inclusion and equity on the basis of mission attainment and values rather than legal compliance.
(3) Taking a systems thinking perspective, policymakers and work unit leaders can acknowledge limitations in contemporary diversity approaches and apply research-based knowledge to diagnose diversity shortfalls and persist in addressing unintended effects.
(4) Researchers can employ systems thinking modeling to identify and communicate to others the challenges and necessary scope, timing, persistence, and elaboration of practices for sustained achieving of diversity, inclusion, equity, and performance. Organizational members may achieve the same benefits by modeling their own organizations. The modeling of case studies provides insights on effective change processes and customizing options.
(5) Looking across their various disciplines, scholars can model dynamic systems in their individual studies and in transdisciplinary syntheses of research to generate empirically based knowledge that properly conveys dynamic complexities and the workings over time of practical leverage points.
(6) Forming the detailed dynamic complexities of diversity into a single systems thinking model proved beyond our capabilities and may be unnecessary for guiding effective policies. Rather, simplified overview models and

more detailed breakout sub-models, as presented earlier, may provide adequate guidance for the persistent, customized policy revision necessary for any one organization.

To the knowledge produced by a dynamic systems perspective on diversity research, organizational policymakers can add local knowledge of their organization and its members (Rousseau, 2012), periodically gathering feedback, diagnosing dynamics causing diversity policy resistance in their settings, and using the resulting insights to revise and implement their policies. In doing so, they may choose to augment scholarly produced knowledge by utilizing participatory model-building exercises that draw on organizational members' knowledge of their immediate systems. Cases of participatory model-building have been described and analyzed in system dynamics literature (Rouwette et al., 2011; Vennix, 1999), including a case study focused on inclusion (Trani et al., 2019). In large organizations participatory model-building can occur within work units.

As illustrated by the science unit and medical research unit cases (Section 9), allowing experimentation and variation within the organization to accommodate differing unit purposes and characteristics confers the resiliency of self-organizing emphasized by Meadows (2008), enabling managers and workgroup members to evolve inclusive practices that work for their unit. Principal means are providing a range of relevant information and supporting timely experimentation, encouraging movement away from attempts to tightly control their system by relying solely on prescriptive outcomes accountability policies. Belief in a singular way to achieve diversity with inclusion and performance should be challenged, enabling variability and pursuit of better alternatives that fit the work unit's context. The "natural" variability in how organizations evolve and function enabled us to find some organizations, such as the service fraternity, that have achieved sustained diversity, inclusion, and equity, whether those were intentional goals or not, through self-evolution in pursuit of performance or their missions.

These conclusions suggest that systems modeling of diversity phenomena can be of value to both researchers and organizational members. Future research studies can continue the efforts to probe and model the unintended, follow-on effects of a variety of diversity policies. Studies can also inquire into leverage points that mitigate the dynamics reproducing exclusion, inequity, and diminished performance. In particular, more field research should inquire into the determinants of intergroup interactions that are inclusive, given the surprising infrequency of organizations and diversity researchers applying concepts of intergroup contact to achieve productive interactions. Further, and perhaps of greatest value, systems modeling provides a tool for scholars to synthesize in causal loop diagrams the empirical findings generated by many academic disciplines, producing evidence-based models that communicate to organizational leaders' insights into dealing successfully with diversity's dynamic complexities.

The many academic disciplines studying diversity phenomena have lacked a system perspective enabling them to investigate dynamics driving the reproduction of diversity problems over time. In our case the overarching framework was developed over several years, drawing on a program of research involving thematic analysis of interviews in qualitative studies, data analysis in quantitative studies, synthesis of literature reviews from several academic disciplines, and collection and analysis of organizational cases, as detailed in Bernstein et al., 2022. Much literature has identified the value of understanding system dynamics and virtuous and vicious feedback loops to diagnose the behavior of a system and, for policy action, identifying leverage points to support positive change and limit negative change (Barlas, 2007; Hovmand et al., 2012; Rouwette et al., 2011; Sterman, 2006; Vennix, 1999). Here, applying systems thinking modeling enabled a deeper look into the positive and negative components affecting the attainment of sustainable inclusion, equity, and work unit performance over time. The research and systems modeling processes enabled us to identify the feedback loops that positively or negatively amplify change over time, creating virtuous or vicious cycles.

Though based on systematic reviews of empirical studies, on high quality individual studies, and on comparative analyses of cases from nonprofit and public sector organizations, our systems thinking-based modeling of the virtuous dynamics of four sets of practices for inclusion, equity, and performance cannot be claimed to be definitive. Rather, we offer the modeling with the aim of stimulating organizational leaders, educators, and researchers to focus on these new, evidence-informed approaches to diverse workforces, approaches whose essence is structuring inclusive practices for successful intergroup engagement.

Recent research on intended and unintended dynamic effects of contemporary policies offers hope that more inquiry and policy practice will deploy and benefit from a dynamic systems perspective. We invite those who have applied system dynamics and systems thinking to complex problems in other fields to help in guiding its application to issues of diversity, equity, inclusion, and performance. We invite organizational leaders whose organizations have achieved sustained inclusion, equity, and superior mission attainment to share their knowledge in a fashion that conveys diversity's dynamic complexities and possibilities.

References

Ahmad, F., & Barner-Rasmussen, W. (2019). False foe? When and how code switching practices can support knowledge sharing in multinational corporations. *Journal of International Management*, *25*(3), 100671.

Allport, G. W. (1954). *The Nature of Prejudice*. Addison-Wesley.

Amis, J. M., Mair, J., & Munir, K. A. (2020). The organizational reproduction of inequality. *Academy of Management Annals*, *14*(1), 195–230.

Barlas, Y. (2007). System dynamics: Systemic feedback modeling for policy analysis. *System*, *1*(59), 1–68.

Bauer, T. N., Bodner, T., Erdogan, B., Truxillo, D. M., & Tucker, J. S. (2007). Newcomer adjustment during organizational socialization: A meta-analytic review of antecedents, outcomes, and methods. *Journal of Applied Psychology*, *92*(3), 707.

Bear, A., Colwell, R. R., & Helman, A. (Eds.). (2020). *Promising Practices for Addressing the Underrepresentation of Women in Science, Engineering, and Medicine: Opening Doors*. National Academies Press. https://doi.org/10.17226/25585.

Becker, G.S. (1971). *The Economics of Discrimination* (2nd Ed.). University of Chicago Press.

Bernstein, R. S., & Aspin, T. (2024). Cascade public media. *Journal of Nonprofit Education and Leadership*, *14*(2), 17–41.

Bernstein, R. S., & Salipante, P. (2015). Comfort versus discomfort in inter-racial/interethnic interactions: Group practices on campus. *Equality, Diversity and Inclusion: An International Journal*, *34*(5), 376–394.

Bernstein, R. S., & Salipante, P. (2017, July). Intercultural comfort through social practices: Exploring conditions for cultural learning. *Frontiers in Education, 2*, 31. Frontiers Media SA.

Bernstein, R. S., & Salipante, P. F. (2024). Diversity and inclusion in nonprofit organizations. In D. O. Renz and Associates (Eds.), *The Jossey-Bass Handbook of Nonprofit Leadership and Management 5th Edition.* Jossey-Bass.

Bernstein, R. S., Salipante, P. F., & Weisinger, J. W. (2022). *Performance Through Diversity and Inclusion: Leveraging Organizational Practices for Equity and Results*. Routledge. https://doi.org/10.3389/feduc.2017.00031.

Bertrand, M., & Duflo, E. (2017). Field experiments on discrimination. *Handbook of Economic Field Experiments*, *1*, 309–393.

Boin, J., Rupar, M., Graf, S. et al. (2021). The generalization of intergroup contact effects: Emerging research, policy relevance, and future directions. *Journal of Social Issues*, *77*(1), 105–131.

Bourdieu P., (1977), *Outline of a Theory of Practice* (translated by Nice Richard), Cambridge: Cambridge University Press.

Bourdieu, P. (2020). Outline of a theory of practice. In Steven Seidman and Jeffrey C. Alexander (Eds.), *The New Social Theory Reader*: 80–86. Routledge.

Bowman, N. A. (2013). How much diversity is enough? The curvilinear relationship between college diversity interactions and first-year student outcomes. *Research in Higher Education*, *54*, 874–894.

Brannon, T. N., Carter, E. R., Murdock-Perriera, L. A., & Higginbotham, G. D. (2018). From backlash to inclusion for all: Instituting diversity efforts to maximize benefits across group lines. *Social Issues and Policy Review*, *12*(1), 57–90.

Buckman, S.R., Choi, L. Y., Daly, M. C., & Seitelman. L. M. (2021). The economic gains from equity, Federal Reserve Bank of San Francisco Working Paper 2021–11. https://doi.org/10.24148/wp2021-11.

Buse, K., Bernstein, R. S., & Bilimoria, D. (2016). The influence of board diversity, board diversity policies and practices, and board inclusion behaviors on nonprofit governance practices. *Journal of Business Ethics*, *133*, 179–191.

Cable, D. M., Gino, F., & Staats, B. R. (2013). Breaking them in or eliciting their best? Reframing socialization around newcomers' authentic self-expression. *Administrative Science Quarterly*, *58*(1), 1–36.

Caleo, S., & Heilman, M. E. (2019). What could go wrong? Some unintended consequences of gender bias interventions. *Archives of Scientific Psychology*, *7*(1), 71.

Carr, P. L., Gunn, C. M., Kaplan, S. A., Raj, A., & Freund, K. M. (2015). Inadequate progress for women in academic medicine: Findings from the National Faculty Study. *Journal of Women's Health*, *24*(3), 190–199.

Castellaneta, F., Conti, R., & Kacperczyk, A. (2020). The (un) intended consequences of institutions lowering barriers to entrepreneurship: The impact on female workers. *Strategic Management Journal*, *41*(7), 1274–1304.

Castilla, E. J. (2008). Gender, race, and meritocracy in organizational careers. *American Journal of Sociology*, *113*(6), 1479–1526.

Castilla, E. J. (2015). Accounting for the gap: A firm study manipulating organizational accountability and transparency in pay decisions. *Organization Science*, *26*(2), 311–333.

Castilla, E. J., & Benard, S. (2010). The paradox of meritocracy in organizations. *Administrative Science Quarterly, 55*(4), 543–676.

Center for American Progress (2012). The Costly Business of Discrimination Report. www.americanprogress.org/article/the-costly-business-of-discrimin ation/.

Churchman, C. W. M. S. (1967). West. 1967. "Wicked Problems." *Management Science, 14*(4), 141–142.

Daly, M., Hobijn, B., & Pedtke, J. H. (2017). Disappointing facts about the black-white wage gap. *FRBSF Economic Letter, 26*, 1–5.

Dobbin, F., & Kalev, A. (2016). Why diversity programs fail. *Harvard Business Review, 94*(7), 14.

Dobbin, F., Schrage, D., & Kalev, A. (2015). Rage against the iron cage: The varied effects of bureaucratic personnel reforms on diversity. *American Sociological Review, 80*(5), 1014–1044.

Dover, T. L., Kaiser, C. R., & Major, B. (2020). Mixed signals: The unintended effects of diversity initiatives. *Social Issues and Policy Review, 14*(1), 152–181.

Dybå, T., & Dingsøyr, T. (2008). Empirical studies of agile software development: A systematic review. *Information and Software Technology, 50*(9–10), 833–859.

Ely, R. J., & Thomas, D. A. (2001). Cultural diversity at work: The effects of diversity perspectives on work group processes and outcomes. *Administrative Science Quarterly, 46*(2), 229–273.

Evans, L. L., Kuenzi, K., & Stewart, A. J. (2024). A function of board diversity? Does diversity equip nonprofit performance. *Public Administration Quarterly, 49*(1), 20–33. 07349149241281956.

Festinger, L. (1962). *A Theory of Cognitive Dissonance*. Vol. 2. Stanford University Press.

Forrester, J. W. (1961). *Industrial Dynamics*. The MIT Press.

Forrester, J. W. (1990). *Principles of Systems*. Pegasus Communications.

Greyerbiehl, L., & Mitchell Jr, D. (2014). An intersectional social capital analysis of the influence of historically Black sororities on African American women's college experiences at a predominantly White institution. *Journal of Diversity in Higher Education*, 7(4), 282.

Harrison, D. A., Kravitz, D. A., Mayer, D. M., Leslie, L. M., & Lev-Arey, D. (2006). Understanding attitudes toward affirmative action programs in employment: Summary and meta-analysis of 35 years of research. *Journal of Applied Psychology, 91*(5), 1013.

Hernandez, M. D. (2008). Sisterhood beyond the ivory tower: An exploration of black sorority alumnae membership. In G. S. Parks, Jr. (Ed.), *Black Greek*

Letter Organizations in the Twenty First Century: Our Fight Has Just Begun: 253–272. University of Kentucky Press.

Hewstone, M., & Swart, H. (2011). Fifty-odd years of inter-group contact: From hypothesis to integrated theory. *British Journal of Social Psychology, 50*(3), 374–386.

Hoang, T., Suh, J., & Sabharwal, M. (2022). Beyond a numbers game? Impact of diversity and inclusion on the perception of organizational justice. *Public Administration Review, 82*(3), 537–555.

Hovmand, P. S., Andersen, D. F., Rouwette, E. et al. (2012). Group model-building "scripts" as a collaborative planning tool. *Systems Research and Behavioral Science, 29*(2), 179–193.

Hummel, M., Rosenkranz, C., & Holten, R. (2015). The role of social agile practices for direct and indirect communication in information systems development teams. *Communications of the Association for Information Systems, 36*(1), 15.

Jiang, Z., DeHart-Davis, L., & Borry, E. L. (2022). Managerial practice and diversity climate: The roles of workplace voice, centralization, and teamwork. *Public Administration Review, 82*(3), 459–472.

Jones, K. P., Peddie, C. I., Gilrane, V. L., King, E. B., & Gray, A. L. (2016). Not so subtle: A meta-analytic investigation of the correlates of subtle and overt discrimination. *Journal of Management, 42*(6), 1588–1613.

Joshi, A., & Roh, H. (2009). The role of context in work team diversity research: A meta-analytic review. *Academy of Management Journal, 52*(3), 599–627.

Jung, H., & Welch, E. W. (2022). The impact of demographic composition of social networks on perceived inclusion in the workplace. *Public Administration Review, 82*(3), 522–536.

Kalev, A. (2009). Cracking the glass cages? Restructuring and ascriptive inequality at work. *American Journal of Sociology, 114*(6), 1591–1643.

Kalev, A., Dobbin, F., & Kelly, E. (2006). Best practices or best guesses? Assessing the efficacy of corporate affirmative action and diversity policies. *American Sociological Review, 71*(4), 589–617. https://doi.org/10.1177/000312240607100404.

Kauff, M., Beneda, M., Paolini, S. et al. (2021). How do we get people into contact? Predictors of intergroup contact and drivers of contact seeking. *Journal of Social Issues, 77*(1), 38–63.

Kim, J. Y., Fitzsimons, G. M., & Kay, A. C. (2018). Lean in messages increase attributions of women's responsibility for gender inequality. *Journal of Personality and Social Psychology, 115*(6), 974.

Kraus, M. W., Torrez, B., & Hollie, L. (2022). How narratives of racial progress create barriers to diversity, equity, and inclusion in organizations. *Current Opinion in Psychology*, *43*, 108–113.

Kurdi, B., Seitchik, A. E., Axt, J. R. et al. (2019). Relationship between the Implicit Association Test and intergroup behavior: A meta-analysis. *American Psychologist*, *74*(5), 569.

Lee, B. A., Farrell, C. R., & Link, B. G. (2004). Revisiting the contact hypothesis: The case of public exposure to homelessness. *American Sociological Review*, *69*(1), 40–63.

Leslie, L. M., Mayer, D. M., & Kravitz, D. A. (2014). The stigma of affirmative action: A stereotyping-based theory and meta-analytic test of the consequences for performance. *Academy of Management Journal*, *57* (4), 964–989.

Lippens, L., Vermeiren, S., & Baert, S. (2023). The state of hiring discrimination: A meta-analysis of (almost) all recent correspondence experiments. *European Economic Review*, *151*, 104315.

Mabin, V. J., & Cavana, R. Y. (2024). A framework for using Theory of Constraints thinking processes and tools to complement qualitative system dynamics modelling. *System Dynamics Review*, *40*(4), e1768.

Mainiero, L. A., & Gibson, D. E. (2018). The kaleidoscope career model revisited: How midcareer men and women diverge on authenticity, balance, and challenge. *Journal of Career Development*, *45*(4), 361–377.

Marinucci, M., Maunder, R., Sanchez, K. et al. (2021). Intimate intergroup contact across the lifespan. *Journal of Social Issues*, *77*(1), 64–85.

McGee, E. O. (2020). Interrogating structural racism in STEM higher education. *Educational Researcher*, *49*(9), 633–644.

McPherson, M., Smith-Lovin, L., & Cook, J. M. (2001). Birds of a feather: Homophily in social networks. *Annual Review of Sociology*, *27*(1), 415–444.

Meadows, D. H. (2008). *Thinking in Systems: A Primer*. Chelsea Green.

Mowday, R. T. (1991). Equity theory predictions of behavior in organizations. In Porter, L. W., Bigley, G. A., & Steers, R. M (Eds.), *Motivation and Work Behavior*, 5th ed: 111–131.

Museus, S. D., Palmer, R. T., Davis, R. J., & Maramba, D. C. (2011). Racial and ethnic minority students' success in STEM education. *ASHE Higher Education Report*, *36*(6), 1–140.

Nishii, L. H. (2013). The benefits of climate for inclusion for gender-diverse groups. *Academy of Management Journal*, *56*(6), 1754–1774.

Paluck, E. L., Green, S. A., & Green, D. P. (2019). The contact hypothesis re-evaluated. *Behavioural Public Policy*, *3*(2), 129–158.

Paolini, S., White, F. A., Tropp, L. R. et al. (2021). Intergroup contact research in the 21st century: Lessons learned and forward progress if we remain open. *Journal of Social Issues*, *77*(1), 11–37.

Pettigrew, T. F., & Tropp, L. R. (2006). A meta-analytic test of intergroup contact theory. *Journal of Personality and Social Psychology*, *90*(5), 751.

Piatak, J., McDonald, J., & Mohr, Z. (2022). The role of gender in government and nonprofit workplaces: An experimental analysis of rule compliance and trust. *Public Administration Review*, *82*(3), 556–569.

Reckwitz, A. (2002). Toward a theory of social practices: A development in culturalist theorizing. *European Journal of Social Theory*, *5*(2), 243–263.

Repenning, N. P., & Sterman, J. D. (2002). Capability traps and self-confirming attribution errors in the dynamics of process improvement. *Administrative Science Quarterly*, *47*(2), 265–295.

Ross, L. (1977). The intuitive psychologist and his shortcomings: Distortions in the attribution process. In *Advances in Experimental Social Psychology*: 173–220 (Vol. 10). Academic Press.

Rousseau, D. M. (2012). Envisioning evidence-based management. In D. M. Rousseau (Ed.), *The Oxford Handbook of Evidence-Based Management*: 3–24. Oxford University Press.

Rouwette, E. A., Korzilius, H., Vennix, J. A., & Jacobs, E. (2011). Modeling as persuasion: The impact of group model building on attitudes and behavior. *System Dynamics Review*, *27*(1), 1–21.

Sabharwal, M., Levine, H., & D'Agostino, M. (2018). A conceptual content analysis of 75 years of diversity research in public administration. *Review of Public Personnel Administration*, *38*(2), 248–267.

Schäfer, S. J., Kauff, M., Prati, F. et al. (2021). Does negative contact undermine attempts to improve intergroup relations? Deepening the understanding of negative contact and its consequences for intergroup contact research and interventions. *Journal of Social Issues*, *77*(1), 197–216.

Simon, H. A. (1996). *The Sciences of the Artificial*. MIT press.

Staw, B. M. (1976). Knee-deep in the big muddy: A study of escalating commitment to a chosen course of action. *Organizational Behavior and Human Performance*, *16*(1), 27–44.

Sterman, J. D. (2002). Systems Dynamics: Systems thinking and modeling for a complex world. M.I.T. Engineering Systems Division, Working Paper Series, ESD-WP-2003-01.13-ESD Internal Symposium.

Sterman, J. D. (2006). Learning from evidence in a complex world. *American Journal of Public Health*, *96*(3), 505–514.

Tomaskovic-Devey, D., Zimmer, C., Stainback, K. et al. (2006). Documenting desegregation: Segregation in American workplaces by race, ethnicity, and sex, 1966–2003. *American Sociological Review, 71*(4), 565–588.

Trani, J. F., Bakhshi, P., Mozaffari, A. et al. (2019). Strengthening child inclusion in the classroom in rural schools of Pakistan and Afghanistan: What did we learn by testing the system dynamics protocol for community engagement? *Research in Comparative and International Education, 14*(1), 158–181.

Van Knippenberg, D., De Dreu, C. K., & Homan, A. C. (2004). Work group diversity and group performance: an integrative model and research agenda. *Journal of Applied Psychology, 89*(6), 1008.

Vennix, J. A. (1999). Group model-building: Tackling messy problems. *System Dynamics Review: The Journal of the System Dynamics Society, 15*(4), 379–401.

Weisinger, J. Y., & Salipante, P. F. (2000). Cultural knowing as practicing: Extending our conceptions of culture. *Journal of Management Inquiry, 9*(4), 376–390.

Weisinger, J. Y., & Salipante, P. F. (2005). A grounded theory for building ethnically bridging social capital in voluntary organizations. *Nonprofit and Voluntary Sector Quarterly, 34*(1), 29–55.

Weisinger, J. Y., & Salipante Jr, P. F. (2007). An expanded theory of pluralistic interactions in voluntary nonprofit organizations. *Nonprofit Management and Leadership, 18*(2), 157–173.

Cambridge Elements

Public and Nonprofit Administration

About the Series

The foundation of this series are cutting-edge contributions on emerging topics and definitive reviews of keystone topics in public and nonprofit administration, especially those that lack longer treatment in textbook or other formats. Among keystone topics of interest for scholars and practitioners of public and nonprofit administration, it covers public management, public budgeting and finance, nonprofit studies, and the interstitial space between the public and nonprofit sectors, along with theoretical and methodological contributions, including quantitative, qualitative and mixed-methods pieces.

The Public Management Research Association

The Public Management Research Association improves public governance by advancing research on public organizations, strengthening links among interdisciplinary scholars, and furthering professional and academic opportunities in public management.

PMRA
public management research association

Cambridge Elements

Public and Nonprofit Administration

Elements in the Series

Organizing and Institutionalizing Local Sustainability: A Design Approach
Aaron Deslatte

Public Administration and Democracy: The Complementarity Principle
Anthony M. Bertelli and Lindsey J. Schwartz

Redefining Development: Resolving Complex Challenges in a Global Context 2nd edition
Jessica Kritz

Experts in Government: The Deep State from Caligula to Trump and Beyond
Donald F. Kettl

New Public Governance as a Hybrid: A Critical Interpretation
Laura Cataldi

Can Governance be Intelligent?: An Interdisciplinary Approach and Evolutionary Modelling for Intelligent Governance in the Digital Age
Eran Vigoda-Gadot

The Courts and the President: Judicial Review of Presidentially Directed Action
Charles Wise

Standing Up for Nonprofits: Advocacy on Federal, Sector-wide Issues
Alan J. Abramson and Benjamin Soskis

Topics in Public Administration: Perspectives from Computational Social Sciences and Corpus Linguistics
Richard M. Walker, Jiasheng Zhang and Yanto Chandra

Public Service Explained: The Role of Citizens in Value Creation
Greta Nasi, Stephen Osborne, Maria Cucciniello and Tie Cui

Court-Ordered Community Service: The Experiences of Community Organizations and Community Service Workers
Rebecca Nesbit, Su Young Choi and Jody Clay-Warner

Sustainable Inclusion through Performance-Driven Practices: An Evidence-Based, Dynamic Systems Framework
Ruth Sessler Bernstein and Paul Salipante

A full series listing is available at: www.cambridge.org/EPNP

For EU product safety concerns, contact us at Calle de José Abascal, 56–1°,
28003 Madrid, Spain or eugpsr@cambridge.org.

www.ingramcontent.com/pod-product-compliance
Lightning Source LLC
Chambersburg PA
CBHW050051220425
25512CB00004B/216
9781009551564